Up
from the
Water

A Journey of Identity, Grace, and Redemption

Up
from the
Water

TANYA SIMPSON

Front cover design by Claudine Mansour Design
Back cover designs for hardback by Liz Schreiter
Back cover designs for paperback by Claudine Mansour Design
Interior design by Liz Schreiter
Author photos by Bridgette Balmes

Published by Thought Leader Academy Publishing
Thought Leader Academy Publishing
3901 N Kildare Ave
Chicago, Il 60641

Hardcover ISBN: 979-8-9913592-6-9
Paperback ISBN: 979-8-9913592-7-6
Ebook ISBN: 979-8-9922574-7-2

This book is dedicated to my late parents, Clifford "Cliff" and Marilyn "Marty" Simpson, and to my sister Judith "Juju" Simpson, who always believed in me and held space for me to grow into the fullness of the person they saw in me.

Contents

Preface

This isn't the book I was going to write. This isn't the path I intended to take. At 57 years old, I had just retired early from corporate America so that I could fully focus on executing my plan to start and build a thriving consulting business working with leaders and their organizations to help them address the troubling trend of women leaders leaving their companies in record numbers. Women like me.

I had my business teed up and ready to go. I had created LLCs. Registered domain names. Written a business plan. Secured funding. Identified talent. Developed clients. I had even begun a Ph.D. in Organizational Psychology, figuring that my business would be fertile ground for research that, in turn, would bolster my credentials as I sought out meatier corporate engagements. Yep, I had it all figured out.

But then God showed up. Actually, He was there all along, but this time He got my attention. They say, "If you want to make God laugh, tell Him your plans." I guess God must have been having a pretty good belly laugh.

Up to that point, I had lived my life on the surface, comfortably afloat. I had built myself a really nice boat. The kind of boat that gave the appearance of having mastered the sea of life. But in reality, I was adrift. I had somehow managed to weather some nasty storms, but I had simply sailed out of them, with no direction. How could I help anyone else to navigate life's waters while my own sails remained aflutter?

God's answer: I had to leave the surface of the water. Jump overboard. I had to let go of the comfort of my nice, safe boat and dive deep below the surface, untethered. Only by fully immersing myself in the depths of what had gone before could all of the ballast that was no longer serving me be washed away. Only then could I rise up and break through the limitations of the surface to reap the fullness of a life lived above the water.

You'll hear me use the word God quite a bit in this book. I even use the word Jesus a time or two towards the end. Don't let those words bother you. If God and Jesus aren't your jam, that's perfectly fine, this book is still for you. Here's the thing: It would be hypocritical of me to encourage you to be authentic and to shine in your own truth while I myself am hiding mine. My truth includes God and Jesus, so I can't just leave them out. How about you and I make a deal: I'll be authentically me, and you be authentically you, and we can walk through this book together and be kind to one another without anybody getting tripped up over each other's words. Deal?

Good! Now come along with me and I'll tell you a story about a little girl with big dreams who was bound and determined to do it all on her own. A little girl on a grown-up journey who found redemption, completion, and a new heart along the way.

CHAPTER ONE

The Hill

first suspected that things might be worse than I had initially thought when I noticed the blood blooming and spreading on my white canvas shoes. I had bought them specifically for this trip, and I loved those shoes with their shiny metal D-ring eyes and their trendy round toes. I thought that they made me look cool. Hip. Popular. All of which I was not. As the blood poured from my mouth onto the toes of my shoes while I sat by the side of the road waiting for someone to come along, the full gravity of the situation washed over me all at once as my tongue encountered something out of place deep inside my mouth and recognized it as my teeth. My front teeth. *Oh my God, my teeth! What are they doing back here?!*

It was 1985, the summer between high school and college, and I had been on my way to brass camp. This was a camp for top young trumpet, trombone, French horn and tuba talent from all over the world, and it would have been my third and final year there before heading off to the University of Southern California with a scholarship to study jazz trombone.

It was also my first time driving solo "over the hill." That's what we called it in the San Francisco Bay Area when you traversed the Santa Cruz mountains on the narrow, winding roads that connect what is now known as Silicon Valley to the Pacific Ocean. I was looking forward to showing off my new-to-me 1964 Ford Falcon convertible. I had spied the "For Sale" sign peeking out of the windshield in the bank parking lot and knew immediately that this metallic blue embodiment of raw power would be my first car. It was different from anything that I had seen in the high school parking lot. It would attract attention. Good attention. It was affordable. And it reminded me of my friend Renée's car.

Renée was a really, really good trumpet player. I had met her at brass camp two years before. She was a couple of years older than me, already in her second year of college as a music major, and she was cool. Fun. Popular. Boys liked her. She was the kind of person that I wanted to be. And, incomprehensibly, Renée was my friend. And Renée would be at brass camp.

Everybody at brass camp knew Renée, and everybody knew Renée's car – a baby blue fifty-seven Chevy Bel Air. I'm not sure if anybody had ever noticed that Renée and I were friends. Maybe if people saw that I had a car like Renée's, they would notice me, too. In a good way.

Mom and Dad had begged me to let them drive me over the hill to camp, but I had insisted that I was perfectly capable of driving myself. I was almost an adult now! I had my driver's license and had been driving for over a year. I had my own car. I had a scholarship to college. I had survived numerous band and orchestra trips without my mom or dad tagging along. Most of the other musicians at camp would be adults. Cool adults! And I'll be damned if they were going to see me being dropped off at camp by my parents.

The story that I told afterwards was not what actually happened. I told a story about a car coming around the corner from the opposite direction in its own lane and a motorcycle coming around that same corner in mine. That left me with a split second and four bad options: over the side of the cliff to my left, head-on into the car, head-on into the motorcycle, or into the side of the hill on my right. I ended up going into the side of the hill. My mother would later tell me that they got the guy, further down the road. The motorcyclist who had been passing the other car on a blind turn.

So, what actually happened? I was terrified driving on that road. This winding, two-lane mountain road was nothing like the broad city streets in my neighborhood. I had realized pretty quickly that I was in over my head, but there was no place to turn around, or at least no place that I was comfortable turning around, so I kept going. Before long, a motorcycle came along, right up behind me. A racing-style motorcycle that was clearly not interested in creeping over the hill at the pace that I was driving. And there was a whole lot of hill left to go.

I kept looking in my rear view mirror at that bike. Staring at it as it sped up and braked and leaned and dipped back and forth behind me. I didn't know at the time that it was simply warming up its tires for the ride. I imagined the frustration that rider must have been feeling. Frustration toward me. I was in the way. An obstacle. An object. I felt the inadequacy of my own abilities. The shame of not being a better driver. Of not being good enough. *What must they think of me? They must think that I'm an idiot. They're right, I am an idiot. They must think that I don't belong here. They're right, I don't belong here. I don't belong anywhere. They must wish that I didn't exist.*

Then a car did come around the corner in its own lane. But unlike the story that I told, there was no motorcycle passing it in mine. When I looked ahead and saw that car coming around the corner, I also saw that it was I who had drifted into the other lane while I was looking in the rear view mirror, obsessed with what the rider behind me must be thinking. What they must be thinking about me.

I remember panicking when I saw that oncoming car. I remember pulling hard to steer out of its path. I remember overcorrecting. I remember heading for the side of the hill, fast. I remember not braking. I remember a strange feeling of calm come over me as I closed in on the side of the hill. I remember letting go, surrendering to the inevitable.

And the next thing I remember is waking up, stopped.

So, the part about where I ended up is true. And because cars built in 1964 were not built to the same standards as cars built twenty years later, a few things made matters worse than they needed to be. One is that the seatbelt was only a lap belt, so there was nothing holding me to the back of the seat. The other is that the seat itself became detached from the rest of the car. And because airbags weren't widely adopted until the 1990s, the result was a violent face plant by the still-seated me into the steel bar that ran across the top of the windshield, snapping my head backwards and shattering and collapsing my face from my left cheekbone through my jaw. This is not the type of impact that people survive. And yet...

I woke up very clear-headed. I took stock of the situation, matter-of-factly. I knew that I had crashed. I saw that the car was right-side-up, embedded nose-in to the side of the hill, and that I was still seated in it. I moved each of my arms and legs and wiggled my fingers and toes. Nothing felt broken. I heard the "*jay-jay*" squawk of a California scrub jay, but no other sounds, so I knew that I could hear, and I also knew that the car wasn't running. I smelled gas. (That car had always smelled like gas, but I had never bothered to find out why.) I concluded that the car was likely not drivable. It occurred to me that it would probably be a good idea to turn off the ignition switch anyway, maybe keep the car from exploding or catching on fire. And so, I did what any normal person would do, in any normal situation, alone with a broken-down car. I turned the ignition switch to the off position, unfastened my lap belt, pulled the keys out of the ignition and put them in my pocket, opened the door, got out of the car, closed the door, walked to the back of the car, and sat down by the side of the road to wait for help.

This wasn't the first time that I should not have survived. When my mom was pregnant with me, the practice of determining a baby's gender *in utero* was not yet mainstream. The technology was new, the image quality was crude and often inconclusive, and much of society was wary of the safety of harnessing power designed to track submarines and laser-focusing it on a still-developing fetus. But the technology had fanned the flames of an industry that capitalized on commercializing the pre-ordination of colors, roles, and destinies that would be assigned to little boys and girls, and my parents were fully bought-in.

Whether they didn't get an ultrasound or whether they got one that was inconclusive, I don't know, but I was so active and kicked so strongly in the womb that my parents were convinced that I was going to be a boy. They painted my room blue, bought baby boy outfits and toys, and imagined what their little boy's life would be like. The adventures that my dad and I would have together. The sports that I would play. What I would be when I grew up. Maybe a doctor or a lawyer.

Cliff and Marty Simpson considered, weighed, sifted, and rejected various baby boy names. Charles, after my paternal grandfather? Clyde, after my maternal grandfather and my mother's brother? Clifford Jr.? No, they would not name me after anyone else. They wanted me to be my own person. My dad really liked the name Joaquín, after the San Joaquín Valley in central California where he spent his formative years on his grandparents' farm. But no amount of Dad's advocating for Joaquín made any headway at all with my mother. Joaquín was a hard "no" for my mom, who grew up in a family where names like Joaquín belonged to laborers and servants who worked under families like hers. Lower class people. Lesser people. My parents eventually settled on the name Curt for me, sticking with the "C" theme of Clifford, Charles, and Clyde, but choosing for me a name all my own, wanting me to blaze a path that hadn't been traveled before.

After nine uneventful months of gestation and over fourteen hours of labor, their little blue baby came into this world. I was not the kind of blue that my parents had had in mind. I didn't cry. I tried to breathe, but I wasn't getting any air. The doctors quickly whisked me away to the NICU and placed me in an incubator surrounded by an oxygen tent. Tests would soon reveal that my lungs were under-developed, and one of them wouldn't open. The odds of my survival were not good, and even if I did survive, I would likely be brain-damaged and experience health complications for the rest of my life. The next few days would be crucial.

"Oh, and also, Mr. and Mrs. Simpson, it's a girl."

For the next week, my parents took turns in the NICU, never leaving my side. They would slide their hands into the thick gloves that reached inside of that oxygen tent and caress my head and whatever parts of my small body that they could find in between the tubes and the patches and the wires. They would talk to me. Sing to me. Read to me. And they would pray. Oh, how they prayed.

"Dear God, if you can hear us, if there is any chance at all that this baby can survive, we will keep her, we will love her, we will take care of her, and we will raise her in the church. Please God, hear our prayer."

And then, one morning, I cried. It started out as a gulpy, hesitant whimper, but it quickly crescendoed to the loudest, fullest cry in that NICU. My parents cried. The nurses cried. The doctors cried. And I, too, just kept right on crying. The room was a chorus of cries! Within a few days, my parents were taking their now pink, little baby home. Their pink, little baby girl.

The better part of an hour had passed before the ambulance made it up the hill to where I had crashed. Cellular phones in 1985 were big and heavy and expensive, and almost no one had one, so either someone with a CB radio had reported the crash, or someone had driven to find a pay phone to call it in. In the meantime, three motorists had stopped to help me. One was a registered nurse who was doing her best to stop the bleeding. The second proclaimed that he knew CPR and was challenging the nurse over which of them was more qualified to render aid. The third was grabbing ice out of the beer cooler in the back of his pickup truck. When the ambulance finally arrived, I was hastily strapped to a gurney and loaded up into that wagon like freight, and then we were off, sirens blaring, speeding back down the hill the same way that I had come.

I remember the paramedic in the back asking me all sorts of questions. "What's your name?" she asked. "Do you know where you are?" "What's your phone number?" "Do you know what day it is today?" Meanwhile, I was on my back, strapped down, unable to speak, drowning in my own blood. I was fighting to sit up so that I could breathe, but the paramedic kept pushing me back down, telling me to relax. "Try to stay calm, sweetie," she urged.

She didn't understand what I was straining to communicate. *I have to sit up! I'm drowning! I can't breathe!* Somehow, I summoned the strength to bust through those straps, overpower the well-meaning paramedic, and get myself up onto my hands and knees. Blood gushed from my mouth and throat, and I coughed and coughed. She understood now. I motioned for a piece of paper and a pen, and I wrote down my name and phone number.

As we zigged and zagged and jostled down that winding mountain road, me on my elbows and knees, head in hands, I began to get drowsy. I knew from watching the TV drama, *Emergency!*, that this wasn't good. You have to keep accident victims awake, I had learned. Oh, no, this was not good at all. So, I started to pray The Lord's Prayer in my head. My parents had indeed raised me in the church, along with my younger sister, just like they had promised that they would, and I knew The Lord's Prayer like I knew my own name. I wasn't quite sure what it all meant, but by God I knew all the words!

Except not that day. I would start reciting the prayer and get about three or four lines into it and then forget how the rest of it went. Frustrated at my inability to remember something that I knew so well, I would start over, and I would get stuck again, this time earlier. Determined to stay awake, I just kept getting as far as I could, then starting over. And over. And over. Each time getting less and less far. By the time that we got to the hospital, I was down to just, "Our Father…"

I don't remember a whole lot more about that day. I remember my parents rushing into the ER where I was sitting up in a curtained-off bed, throwing up in a pan. I remember the doctor talking about surgery. I remember my parents being more than willing to sign whatever papers were shoved in front of them. I remember being wheeled away to the OR. I remember the anesthesiologist hurriedly putting me under. I remember that process playing out in the wrong order, with my heart and lungs stopping first, while I was still awake, instead of the other way around. I remember desperately trying to kick my legs to gain someone's attention. Trying to get anyone to notice that my heart and lungs had just quit. That I may have just died. And I remember, in the final moment before I lost consciousness, knowing for certain that I had unfinished business left to do. That I still had some sort of assignment to carry out before I went to meet Our Father.

CHAPTER TWO

My Instrument

The summer following my accident was full of prayers, surgeries, wired jaws, liquified meals, and lots and lots of nurturing by my mom. Thankfully, other than a badly split lower lip, I had somehow managed to avoid lacerations to my face. But beneath the surface, my lower jaw, palate, and left cheekbone were cratered and broken into more pieces than anyone could count. Had I hit the top of the windshield an inch or two lower, my eyes and nose would have been smashed. An inch or two higher, and my neck would have broken. Either I had gotten remarkably lucky, or someone had been watching over me.

Throughout those summer months, I remained stubbornly determined to enroll in the Jazz Studies program at USC as planned. Never mind that I had a gaping hole in my smile where nine of my front teeth used to be. Never mind that I couldn't play the instrument that the university was paying me to study. Never mind that my well-meaning parents were encouraging me to wait a year so that I could fully heal, wanting to protect me from failure and from the rejection that would no doubt come from showing up as a college freshman with a face that looked like Humpty Dumpty. I had decided, as has always been my nature, to blow past everything and everyone that was telling me that I couldn't do this and to just keep going, trusting that whatever I needed would catch up if I just didn't quit. So in August of 1985, right on schedule, I loaded my trombone, a few books, and all of my clothes into the silver Datsun 210 that had been my father's commuter car, hugged my parents goodbye, hopped right back up into the saddle, and drove my Humpty Dumpty self the six-and-a-half hours south on Interstate 5 to Los Angeles.

In some ways, everything did catch up. I was fitted for a new smile a couple of weeks into the semester, and I immediately immersed myself into the Herculean task of teaching my mouth how to play the trombone again. For those who have never played a wind instrument, the sound that comes out of the listening end of the instrument is fundamentally shaped by how the human interacts with the mouth end of the instrument. Because the characteristics of each person's mouth are unique, like a fingerprint, each person's sound is unique, in much the same way as each person's voice is unique. At first, I couldn't make a sound, any sound, which was frightening. But I worked and worked and worked and worked and was eventually able to sustain a strong, quality tone through full practice sessions.

I joined USC's concert band as a place to begin rebuilding my chops, and I was able to hold my own as a solid section player. However, while I had rebuilt my ability to play, the unique sound that I had had before the accident, the sound that was so attractive in the jazz world that it had earned me a scholarship to a prestigious jazz studies program, was gone. I sounded ordinary, which in the music world means that I was interchangeable. Replaceable. Dispensable. And in the arts world, where only a fraction of the top one percent breaks out and makes a good living, this meant that for me, music – the love of my life for my entire life thus far – could now at best be only a side hustle. The university noticed the change, too, and by the end of the semester, I was informed that I was welcome to stay on as a music major, but that my jazz studies scholarship would not be renewed.

I was devastated. Music had not just been my first love, it had been my identity. And now, at the tender age of eighteen, it was gone.

Music had defined my life since probably before I was born. My maternal grandmother was an Eastman-schooled concert pianist, and my mother sang and played piano her whole life. I can't remember a time when music was not playing in my childhood home, whether it was coming from my parents' living room speakers or from my mother's piano. Mom sang in a local women's choir at the YWCA called the *Y-Zingers*, and she also accompanied all our local schools' musicals on the piano. This meant lots and lots of practice. So much practice that my sister and I would escape to our friends' houses just to not have to hear the same pieces played over and over again, day after day.

As a child, I was sick quite a lot. No matter what bug I caught – and I seemed to catch them all – it would turn into bronchitis or pneumonia. On top of all of that, I had asthma. I still remember the day that our fifth grade class was scheduled to complete the 600-yard walk-run as part of the Presidential Fitness Test. In the 1960s and 70s, all United States children were tested for fitness in school. Something to do with President Kennedy's concerns that the softness of American children was jeopardizing the vitality of the nation.[1]

It was a hot, humid, Friday afternoon, the field had just been mowed for the occasion, and I was allergic to grass. I told the teacher in charge that I wasn't supposed to be on grass, especially freshly-mowed grass, but she didn't believe me. She thought that I was making that up to get out of the test. So, I lined up obediently with the rest of the fifth-graders and ran around the grass course until I couldn't breathe, and then I stumbled my way off of the field, gasping for air. The teacher sent me to the nurse's office, and the school sent me home. By the time that I had walked the single block from the school to my house, I was blue. My mom and dad rushed me to the hospital, and after being given oxygen and a shot of epinephrine, I was back to being pink again.

I would not have wanted to be an administrator at that school on the following Monday when my parents let those administrators have a

---

1   *See* Kennedy, John F. (December 26, 1960). "Sport on the New Frontier: The Soft American", *Sports Illustrated*, Vol. 13, Issue 26, p. 14-17.

piece of their mind! After all of the fear that had surrounded my arrival into this world, and given my resulting fragile health, my parents were extremely protective of me. They did everything in their power to avoid placing me in situations where there was any kind of risk to my health whatsoever. School was supposed to be a trustworthy place, a place where children were safe. Not only had the school put my health in danger by failing to excuse me from the 600-yard walk-run, they had exacerbated the situation by sending me to walk home alone while I was clearly struggling to breathe.

During all of the days that I spent at home, sick, music was a constant. My parents' stereo. Mom practicing. And my record player. I had a Fisher-Price record player as a small child, and then, when I was in the first grade, my dad bought me my own real record player that played real records. I had 33s (the big albums with the little hole) and 45s (the little singles with the big hole), and sometimes I would sneak into my parents' record cabinet and poach their older 78s. Tommy Dorsey. Glenn Miller. Count Basie. Benny Goodman. Louis Armstrong. Ella Fitzgerald. Billie Holliday. The list went on. I would sit on the floor of my bedroom with staff paper that I had "borrowed" from my mom, listening to records, and I would transcribe my favorite licks and riffs from sound to paper. It didn't occur to me until later in life that this was unusual. I just assumed that all children did that.

One day, in fifth-grade, my classmates and I were given a flyer to take home to our parents. The owner of the local music store was coming to our K-through-6 school for an assembly with fifth- and sixth-graders, and parents were invited. He was going to bring instruments for us to try. We could pick out any instrument that we liked, and we could take it home. The school was going to start a band! I was so excited that I ran home from school that day as fast as my legs would go. I burst through the front door, and I begged my mother to let me play an instrument in the band. I could tell that she really wanted to say yes, but musical instrument rental was expensive, and our family was already stretched.

"We'll have to ask your father when he gets home," she said.

In my experience as a child, this was code for "no."

Every minute waiting for my father to come home felt like an hour. I don't even think he had both feet in the door when I ambushed him with the flyer.

"Please, oh please, Daddy," I begged. "Please can I play an instrument in the band?"

To my surprise, my father acquiesced. This was a big deal, because I had never been allowed to participate in any group activities at school. That was probably because most of them were sports, which would have risked aggravating my asthma. But the combination of that plus being sick all the time meant that I had spent much of my childhood feeling socially isolated. I made sure that my mother posted the flyer on the refrigerator so that we would remember which day the music store man was coming. I looked at that flyer every day, the excitement building. I was going to have an instrument to play! Maybe a flute or a violin! And I was going to be in a band!

When assembly day finally arrived, I woke up with a sore throat and a high fever. I was so disappointed! I cried and cried and begged my parents to pleeeeeease let me go to school anyway. I had to get my instrument! I just had to be in that band! Of course, I didn't get to go to school that day, or the next day, or for a whole week afterwards, but, mercifully, my mom had called the school on assembly day, and they had agreed to save an instrument for me.

When I finally got back to school, my teacher told me that my instrument was waiting for me in the office and that I could pick it up there at the end of the day. I packed up my backpack early, and the second the bell rang, I ran from my classroom straight to the office. I hadn't brought anything extra to school that day to make sure that there would be room in my backpack for my instrument. What would it be? Would it be a flute? A clarinet? A violin? I figured that I could probably fit a violin in my backpack if I left the zipper open at the top.

When the school secretary brought my instrument out from the nurse's office and presented it to me with a big smile, I was stunned. The case was enormous! It was *way* too big to fit into my backpack. After all of the other kids had picked out their flutes and their clarinets and their trumpets and their saxophones, the instrument that was left over, the one that nobody had wanted, was a trombone. A trombone? The one with the big slidey thing that I had seen on TV when I had watched *The Lawrence Welk Show* with my parents? That was my instrument?! Nevertheless, it only took me a minute to get over the initial shock. I don't remember if I even looked inside the case. I had an instrument! Who cares if it was nearly as big as I was. It was mine, and I was taking it home!

From the day that I got that trombone, I had something that I excelled in. I was a natural musician, and the trombone gave me an outlet to develop that. I earned first-chair in every band and jazz group in my school. I traveled to Europe with another high-school's orchestra to compete in an international competition. I rode the county transit bus from my high school to one local community college twice a week to play in their jazz band, and to another once a week to play in their orchestra. I took college-level summer music classes at the local university. I was selected for county honor bands. State honor bands. National honor bands and orchestras. I won awards at solo and ensemble competitions and amassed a room full of certificates, ribbons and trophies that rivaled any of my classmates who excelled in sports. I even started my own jazz combo in high school that played actual paying gigs.

But more importantly for me, for the first time in my young life, people knew who I was. They noticed me, in a good way. I had a name. I was somebody. I was part of a group. People actually wanted me in their group. They picked me first, not last. Inside of my world of music, I had an identity. I belonged somewhere.

Outside of my music world, however, I remained invisible. Or worse. Sometimes people noticed me in a bad way. I was mocked, taunted, and picked-on for being small, sickly, weak, a loner. All of which were true.

CHAPTER THREE

Bright Little Flash in the Pan

At Christmastime in 1985, I loaded that Datsun 210 back up with my trombone, my books, and all of my clothes, drove the six-and-a-half hours north on Interstate 5, and returned home, utterly and completely lost. My first and only semester at USC had ended in shame, and I had no idea who I was or what I was supposed to do now.

My parents never articulated the phrase, "I told you so," but I could sense it lurking in the spaces between the words that they did speak. "Oh, Honey, it's okay. We're proud of you for trying," they said. And they really were proud of me. They had told me that a lot in my life, and they had always meant it. However, as much as that statement was intended as encouragement, it was delivered with a tone of resignation. There was no "Get back in there, you can do it!" or "Keep going, we believe in you!" Instead, "We're proud of you" was usually accompanied by an unspoken "but" followed by a suggestion of something else that I could do that might be easier for me. Something safer. The unsaid "I told you so" wasn't condemnation, it was pity. Their poor daughter had tried and failed. The poor thing needed rescuing. The poor thing needed protecting. Needed redirecting. Needed love.

I did need love, but I railed against the kind of love that came wrapped in pity. Pity was bad attention. Pity implied weakness. Incompetence. Inconsequence. Pity made me an object of someone's love, rather than a participant in it. It was dehumanizing. At a time when I needed a hand up from despair to regain my footing and stand in an identity of my own, pity pushed me back down to being the poor little girl who couldn't so much as breathe on her own, the poor thing who couldn't even exist without the help and protection of someone else. And now, here I was, back in my childhood home, depending on my parents for survival.

My parents did their best to help me in the ways that they knew how. On my father's encouragement, I enrolled in my local university that spring. But lacking any sense of direction, I dropped out after a single semester. The next semester, I enrolled in community college and took a few general education courses, then switched to a different community college, then dropped out again. During all of this, I held various jobs flipping burgers, seating restaurant customers, answering phones, and filing papers. I taught myself how to type from a library book so that I could make an additional few cents per hour. Anything to prove that I still had value. That I was still somebody.

One job that I took was answering the phone and taking messages at the front desk of a stock brokerage firm that served as a market-maker for penny stocks. Unbeknownst to me at the time, it was a *Wolf of Wall Street* type of operation where the brokerage had ties to a private equity company that would fund tiny, high-risk start-ups and take them public. The brokers would then call people using the white pages of the phone book and would sell that stock to whomever would buy it to pump the stock up, and then they would dump all of the stock belonging to the original investors, making a ton of money for those original investors and for themselves. This of course would cause the stock to tank, and the people from the white pages would lose their money. It was kind of like the tale of *Robin Hood*, only in reverse. I didn't see all of that. I just saw a bunch of hot shot guys making obscene amounts of money and having an outrageously good time.

One day, something unusual happened, something that no one at the brokerage had ever seen before. A female broker was hired. Every eye followed her as she strode across that floor to the far end of the room and took up residence at her assigned desk. She was the only female in the whole operation who was not a clerical worker, and she was drop-dead gorgeous. That part didn't bother any of the guys one bit. What did bother them quite a bit was that she immediately proceeded to run circles around all of them, even the hottest of the hot shots, and she soon rocketed right up to the head of the pack. Watching her, how hard she worked, how successful she was, how confidently she carried herself, a lightbulb came on for me: maybe I could do that.

I asked the managing broker if he would consider letting me give it a try. He laughed. But in the midst of his laughter, he quipped that if I could somehow manage to pass the licensing exams, he would find me a desk. I didn't have the money to take the recommended exam preparation courses, so I borrowed used books from one of the brokers and studied for the exams on my own. When I was ready to take the tests, I went to the managing broker, whose sponsorship was required in order for me to sit for the exams, and I let him know that I was ready. He laughed again. Harder this time. I just stood there. I kept right on standing there until he finally stopped laughing and said, "You're serious, aren't you." Yes, I was serious. He signed my forms. When I brought him the letters stating that I had passed both of the required exams on my first try, he just shook his head, said, "Well, I'll be damned," handed me a phone book, and pointed to an empty desk. "Start calling," he said, and walked away laughing.

From day one, I outpaced everybody, even the rock star female broker. I sold stock to little old ladies, to parents saving for their kids' college tuition, to single moms, to people on welfare, to people with gambling debt, to anybody looking to make a lot of money in a hurry that saw hope in something shiny. And boy, could I make that stock sound shiny! It's easy to make something sound shiny when you believe that it actually is. I sold it to my neighbors, to my friends, and to my parents' friends. I sold it to anyone that I knew and to anyone who knew someone that I knew. I had found a way to excel again. I was somebody again. I belonged somewhere again.

Belonging with a group of stock brokers in the mid-1980s generally meant being around a lot of drugs. And being around a lot of drugs generally resulted in a lot of drugs ending up in you. I was the youngest broker in the firm, and I was soon the only female after the other one abruptly left without explanation. At twenty years old, I could get into bars easily as long as I was with my high-rolling, older, male colleagues. But I was small and couldn't hold alcohol very well, so my colleagues introduced me to cocaine. Cocaine counteracted the barbiturate effects of alcohol, which meant that I could drink longer, which meant that I could hang out with the group longer, which meant that I could continue belonging somewhere. Problem solved. And the cocaine was free to me, courtesy of my male colleagues who saw lots of opportunity in that situation.

It didn't take much cocaine and alcohol to make me easy prey for the pack of hungry wolves. I had never been popular with boys in school, and after my car accident, I had felt anything but beautiful. But the way that these guys were all over me, you would think that I was the most attractive woman who had ever set foot on the planet. Logically, this was bad attention, but emotionally, subconsciously, it felt like good attention. So, I paid the recurring price of membership to run with the pack and keep that good attention coming.

———

By this time, I had already been acquainted with how things tend to play out for young girls when alcohol and drugs mix with opportunity. I had somehow been invited to a frat party during my one semester at USC, and I had had no idea how to begin to fit in with the fraternity and sorority crowd there. A few of that crowd were the children of celebrities, and all of them had cars, wardrobes, and polished appearances that felt way out of my league.

One of the boys at the party had invited me to get out of there with him, and I had jumped at the chance to leave. I was skeptical about having the attention of an older, good-looking college boy. Why on earth would someone like that want to hang out with someone like me? I was baffled, but I sure wasn't going to do anything to screw it up. His name was Rich. He had vodka in his room, which I had never had before. But my parents drank vodka in their martinis, so how bad could it be? Besides, Rich was mixing it with juice. We drank a lot of it. By the end of the night, I was just conscious enough to understand what was happening, just conscious enough to say "no," but not conscious enough to have the wherewithal to enforce that "no." That was my first time being fully physical with a boy. I never saw Rich again after that.

My parents had warned me about boys like Rich. They had warned me to stay away from boys in general, and especially to never, ever be alone with a boy. During all of my teenage years, my parents had only ever had one thing to say about sex with boys: "Don't." It was wrong. The Bible said that you were only ever supposed to have sex with one person, and that person was your spouse, and then only after you were married. There was no further conversation with my parents about why. No further conversation at all. Just the one-word instruction: "Don't." So, I certainly wasn't going to tell them or anybody else about what had happened with Rich. It had been my own fault anyway, I reasoned. I knew better than to be alone with a boy, but I had done it anyway. This wasn't the first time that I had played with fire, and this time, I had gotten burned. I had to own the consequences. Those consequences were bad enough already without heaping my parents' pity on top of them. So, I just stuffed the shame into the recesses of my mind and moved on.

Monday, October 19, 1987, was a crisp autumn day at the stock bro-kerage. The trees were aflame with yellow, orange, pink, and fiery red, a chilling breeze was scattering anything that wasn't battened down, and change was in the air. The morning started out like any other day. We all were working our way through the day's section of the white pages, pounding coffee, pitching stock, and placing orders. What began as a low buzz in the room grew to a rumble, then a roar, then a cacophony of all-out panic. The market went from bad to worse to historically catastrophic over the course of just a couple of hours. The phones were ringing off the hook. "Sell! Sell! Sell!" the callers demanded. The prob-lem was, there were no buyers to be found. Soon, all that any of us could do was to stand there and stare at the Quotron machines as the bottom fell out of every single stock on the market. That day would later be known as "Black Monday," and by percentage, it remains to this day the largest one-day drop in the history of the stock market.

All of my clients lost all of their money that day. My neighbors, my friends, my family, my family's friends, the little old ladies, the parents saving for their kids' college tuition, the people on welfare, the people with gambling debt, all of the people from the white pages – they all lost it all. The market had dropped 22.6%, but the stocks that I had sold to my clients had dropped straight to zero.

I went home that afternoon shell-shocked. How could I have been so naïve as to miss what was actually happening? How could I have gotten wrapped up in something that had gone so wrong? How could I have involved so many people? Had my need for excelling and belong-ing blinded my judgment? Had I seen any signs and chosen to ignore them, or had I just completely failed to notice the signs altogether? I wasn't sure which was worse. And the answer wasn't going to make one lick of difference for my clients.

I fell into the shower to wash that awful day off of me, and I sobbed. I was completely powerless to help any one of my clients. I had nothing to offer them by way of any comfort or hope at all. Every dollar that they had invested was gone, and it wasn't coming back. It was bad enough that I had allowed myself to be seduced in so many ways, but it was unforgivable that I had become an unwitting seductress. I had led every single one of those people straight off of a cliff, and they had followed me willingly. When I crawled out of the shower, I caught a glimpse of myself in the mirror, and what I saw was ugly. This was not who I wanted to be. I would not be this person any longer.

The next day, before the market's opening bell, I submitted my resignation to the brokerage. I didn't call any of my clients. Didn't get back in there and try to help anyone. Didn't keep going. Instead, I did what pity had taught me: I gave up when things got hard. I just quit. I resigned myself to find something that I could do that was easier. Safer. Better suited to someone like me. I can still hear the words that the managing broker spoke to me as I handed him my letter. "It's too bad," he said. "You were a bright little flash in the pan."[2]

---

2 Not long thereafter, that brokerage was sued in nearly every state, repeatedly sanctioned for a litany of violations, and ultimately expelled from NASD.

CHAPTER FOUR

The Beast

When I left the brokerage, I was once again lost. I had thought that I had found something to excel in, someplace to belong, but as with music, it had ended in shame. Shame revolving around the outcome for my clients, and even more shame revolving around my own behavior and who I had become. I had gotten so caught up in doing whatever it took to fit in with the guys that I had sacrificed my character and dignity in the process.

I was desperate for redemption. For some sort of normalcy and stability. And for that, I turned to an older man whom I had met during my last semester of high school. His name was Luke, and Luke had been thirty years old when I was seventeen. Luke worked at the local music store, and we had met at a jazz competition that the music store had put on for local high school bands. Luke had noticed me, in a good way. He had appreciated my musical talent and had connected me with the recruiter who had ultimately offered me the jazz scholarship to USC.

Luke had also taken an interest in me personally. After my high school graduation, Luke and I had spent a lot of time together, often driving over the hill to hang out on the beaches near Santa Cruz. After my car accident, Luke had been the first person outside of my family to come to my side. He would visit me every day, first in the hospital, and then at home, bringing his guitar and singing songs and sharing stories to cheer me up. As hideously ugly as I felt, Luke made me feel wanted, even loved. As soon as I was up to it, Luke began taking me to the beach again. He made life feel so very normal at a time when it had felt anything but. I needed normalcy now, and Luke was there.

In support of my one-word sex education from my parents while in high school, my mother had provided me with two role models for me to follow: the next door neighbor's daughter, who had married a young pastor right out of college, and our family friends' daughter, Betsy, who was in her late twenties and who had just married a fine husband herself. These were two prime examples of how to choose a husband, according to my mother. I should be on the lookout for a husband like theirs.

I liked the next door neighbor's daughter. I liked Betsy, too. They both had babysat my sister and me when we were young. I looked up to them. I trusted their judgment of what husband material looked like. Luke reminded me of Betsy's husband in both appearance and demeanor. He was also serving as a youth leader at a Lutheran church, the same denomination in which my parents had raised me, and the same denomination as the pastor that the next door neighbor's daughter had married. From what I figured, Luke fit the bill. He was husband material. I figured that if I married a man like Luke, maybe that would atone for the awfulness of my time at the brokerage. Maybe my parents would be proud.

But my parents were not at all happy about this developing situation. As much as I had tried to select good husband material, the thirteen-year age gap was concerning to them. Luke was also recently divorced, which raised additional concerns for my parents. However, Luke had done everything right, including asking my father for my hand in marriage, and my parents were loath to do anything that would risk pushing me away from them. So, my father reluctantly gave Luke my parents' blessing, and at age nineteen, I married the man from the music store.

It wasn't long after the honeymoon before Luke took an interest in other young girls, a situation that came to light when I inquired about the pages of outbound calls to numbers that I didn't recognize that appeared on our phone bill. Between that turn of events and my own emotional wreckage, Luke and I decided to seek the advice of a marriage counselor. One meeting was all that the marriage counselor needed to determine that Luke and I each should seek counseling for our own issues separately, in addition to the marriage counseling.

I had been wary of psychologists before Luke and I even showed up to see the marriage counselor, and now I was being asked to work with two of them. Psychologists were for emotionally frail people, I thought, and the last thing that I needed was someone else pitying me for being frail. But I went along with the sessions anyway, for the sake of my marriage, and I ended up really liking the psychologist who was assigned to me individually. We actually started to dive into real issues, and within a few sessions, I felt myself beginning to drop some barriers and even make a little progress.

And then, one day, the owner of the music store where Luke worked announced that the store would be changing health care plans. Further counseling sessions would no longer be covered. I cried and cried. That psychologist was the first person that I had ever talked with who was willing to listen to everything that I dished up, even the ugliest stuff. Even the parts that were taboo with my parents. He had been willing to work through any issue with me and not pity me and not judge me. I had taken a huge emotional risk and poured out my heart to someone for the first time ever, and we were just getting started, and with one stroke of a businessman's pen, that lifeline was gone. Luke and I didn't have the money to pay for counseling, and we didn't have the tools to navigate the messes that we had made. We hung in there for a little while longer, but within a year of losing our counseling, Luke and I divorced.

With the end of my marriage, I once again returned to my childhood home in the spring of 1989, hat in hand. Once again, I had failed. Once again, my parents took me in. This time, there was no "proud of you" language involved. But no matter what happened in my life, I always knew that I could count on my parents to welcome me home with love and open arms, and they did.

The home where I grew up was nestled on a quiet, residential street in the Almaden Valley of San José, a neighborhood which, at the time, was considered upper-middle-class. Unlike old money, new money, working-middle-class, or chronic poverty, upper-middle-class status did not tend to get passed from generation to generation. Either you went up or you went down. And people in my neighborhood were deathly afraid of going down. The immediate next steps of each family's graduating high school seniors had an outsized role in determining which way that family's next generation went. A pedigree from a good college was a ticket to "up." Consequently, for most families in my neighborhood, college was non-negotiable.

Springtime in the Almaden Valley meant that mailboxes were blooming with letters from colleges – acceptance letters, rejection letters, and the dreaded, anxiety-producing wait-list letters. The neighborhood gossip tree was abuzz with news of where everyone's newly-minted graduates would be going. Attending a local, state-subsidized college was something to be pitied. A consolation prize for those graduating seniors who had failed to gain admission to a more prestigious institution. It was a ticket to "down." This had been ingrained in me throughout my childhood. So, when I re-enrolled in San José State University, after having matriculated through gifted and advanced placement programs all through school, and especially after having done a stint at USC, it was both humbling for me and likely embarrassing for my parents. But such was my lot now, so I was going to make the best of it.

Back at San José State, I bounced around from major to major. I flirted with music for another semester, but the tepid experience was just too heartbreaking. I cycled through "undeclared," English, and even Child Development before landing on a major in Communication Studies, where I excelled in courses like public speaking, persuasion, and organizational communication. Still, despite doing well in those courses and being on track with a solid, academic major at last, there remained an emptiness inside of me that academia just couldn't fill. Music had a hold of my soul, and it refused to let go.

On impulse, after a particularly uninspiring class had adjourned for the day, I decided to walk through the music building instead of veering around it like I usually did. The music building was situated on the way back to my car, and I was just going to pass through it, just this one time, for nostalgia's sake. I had so many fond memories associated with that building from having taken summer courses there during high school and from having performed numerous times on its stage in various honor bands and solo and ensemble competitions.

As I approached the building, a puff of spring breeze infused the air with a sweet fragrance that beckoned me to draw closer. Somewhere in my subconscious, this felt like a bad idea, but I ascended the familiar concrete steps anyway. I lifted a hesitant hand, touched a worn handle, and slipped through the glass door into the lobby of the concert hall. Instantly, I sensed the building stirring, like it knew that I was there. I skirted around the anterior left wing of the concert hall and peeked in through the stage door. The hall was dark, but I could feel the eyes of an unseen audience watching me. Observing. I eased the stage door closed, crept past professors' offices, and ventured warily into the breezeway that connected the front, performance section of the building with the rear, practice section of the building. The breezeway gently ingested me through its belly and emptied me out at the mouth of a hallway lined with dozens of individual practice rooms. And I fell to my knees.

The cacophony of horns and pianos and strings and voices all practicing at once poured out from that hallway and washed over me like a tidal wave. It felt as if I were under water and couldn't see or hear or feel anything beyond all of that chaotic sound. It was deafening. And it was beautiful.

I somehow summoned the strength to rise to my feet, only to find myself dragging one concrete foot, then another, deeper into that hallway of living sound. The hallway drew me further into its bowels and deposited me into an empty practice room. Inside, I closed the door against the beast, turned out the light, dropped to the floor, and bawled. I was in its net now. Music had me. And there would be no more escape.

Figuring out how to navigate a music major without being particularly good at making music was a challenge. Fully committed now, I sank my teeth deep into music history, theory, and composition classes. Music education didn't interest me, but I studied conducting anyway, as well as recording and production. I even learned to play the drums. Anything to stay immersed in music without actually playing the trombone. However, no matter how many avenues that I explored, there was no hiding from the requirement that all music majors must participate in at least one performing ensemble. I eventually capitulated and played third-chair trombone in the concert band in order to comply with that requirement. Trudging through that obligatory exercise in mediocrity was soul-sucking, but I soldiered through for music's sake.

One morning, I was chatting with a classmate while descending the stairs from my second-floor music history class. My classmate's name was Vance, and Vance was on his way to choir rehearsal. Vance mentioned that they were having some sort of a contest that day. To be eligible, he had to bring at least one new singer to rehearsal. I didn't have a class that next hour, so I agreed to tag along with Vance, just for the one rehearsal, so that he could get credit for bringing someone and maybe win a prize. "Great!" Vance said. "Let's go!"

The rehearsal was in Room 150, which was opposite the same hall-way of practice rooms that had devoured me only a few weeks earlier. As Vance and I entered the rehearsal room, Vance turned to the left, found a seat, and sat down. I had assumed that Vance and I would be sitting together, but I noticed that all of the men were sitting on the left side of the room, and all of the women were sitting on the right. I figured that I should probably go right. I looked around and spotted an empty seat way over on the far right side of the room. I made my way over to it and sat down.

All of the students around me seemed to know each other, and they were all talking and hugging and laughing and warming up their voices. I immediately regretted sitting there. What if I had taken somebody's favorite seat? I didn't know anyone, and I certainly wasn't a singer. I didn't belong there. Maybe I should go sit somewhere else. Maybe closer to the back door where we had come in. Closer to the exit. Maybe I should just leave.

As I was plotting my escape, the back door opened. A woman entered the room, strode down the center aisle between the men and the women, and stepped up onto the podium. This must be the direc-tor, I assumed. The woman announced that we would be having sec-tional rehearsals that day, assigned each voice part to a different room, and then dismissed us *en masse* to go rehearse with our sections.

Fantastic! I thought. This would be my opportunity to sneak out, unnoticed.

As everyone filed out of Room 150, I turned to head toward the building exit, but I was abruptly redirected by a student grabbing hold of my arm.

"Soprano rehearsals are this way!" she beamed and pulled me toward the stairs. "My name's Julie, and I'm the soprano section leader. Come with me!"

Apparently, I was not getting out of that rehearsal after all. And, apparently, I was a soprano.

I followed along with Julie and the rest of the sopranos as we herded ourselves back up the same stairs that I had just descended with Vance and into our designated rehearsal room. Once inside, everyone claimed a chair and proceeded to pull the same thick, blue book from their bag. The first thing that I noticed was that the books that everyone was pulling out had over three hundred pages, all of which were filled with music. The second thing that I noticed was that everyone's book was dog-eared and tabbed with multi-colored Post-it notes, and everyone's pages were covered with cryptic-looking pencil markings.

Julie was now standing near the grand piano at the front of the room. The singer next to me leaned over and introduced herself as Tonya. "Tanya!" I replied by way of introduction, pointing to myself. We exchanged smiles, and Tonya invited me to look on with her since I didn't have a thick, blue book of my own. I asked Tonya what song we would be singing. She seemed confused. I pointed to her book. Tonya gave me a quizzical look and replied, "The whole thing." *The whole thing? The whole thing?! All three hundred-plus pages?!!* Tonya must have read my face. "Not all today," she chuckled.

The room bustled as Julie instructed everyone to open their book to a page about three quarters of the way through. Then Julie closed her eyes. The room fell silent. After a moment, Julie opened her eyes, lifted her arms, inhaled deeply, and gestured for us to begin.

"*O Haupt, voll Blut und Wunden,*" the voices sang softly and reverently, "*voll Schmerz und voller Hohn!*" Oh head, full of blood and wounds, full of suffering and full of shame!

The pure yet rich, all-encompassing, unapologetically human sound that Julie coaxed from that room with a few simple gestures of her hands was as achingly profound as the words of the chorale. The most beautiful voices that I had ever heard had begun preparing to perform the passion of the Christ according to St. Matthew, as set to music by Johann Sebastian Bach in 1727. In German. All three-hundred-plus pages of it. Within one line of a single chorus, I was all in.

CHAPTER FIVE

The Summit

Performing Bach's *St. Matthew's Passion* with dual choirs and a period orchestra at Grace Cathedral in San Francisco was like beginning a football career by playing in the Super Bowl. Had I had any inkling of the scope of the undertaking or the caliber of musicians in whose midst I would be singing, I would never have casually followed Vance into Room 150 that day. Not even for a contest. It would have been too intimidating. Thank God for ignorance!

In the three years that I sang with SJSU's Concert Choir and with its chamber choir, the Choraliers, I learned to produce quality vocal sound, sing with understanding in multiple languages, memorize copious amounts of music, work together as one with fellow choristers, trust and follow a conductor, and connect deeply with audiences. I took full advantage of the opportunity to travel extensively with both choirs, performing and competing throughout the country and internationally. I can still feel the collective euphoria of the Choraliers in July of 1991 when it was announced on stage and on broadcast television worldwide that we were the overall winners of the Choir of the World competition – the "Olympics" for choirs – at the International Musical Eisteddfod in Llangollen, Wales.[3]

---

3   The overall winning choir in that same competition in 1955 launched the legendary tenor career of then-19-year-old Luciano Pavarotti.

My experiences with SJSU's choral program filled a lot of holes for me. I was making incredible music, and I belonged somewhere again. In my second year of singing with the Concert Choir, I was elected and served as its President – the first formal vote of confidence that I had ever had from a group of peers. When the paid business manager for the more active Choraliers graduated at the end of that year, I pitched the idea to the director of the music department's choral activities program of expanding the business manager position to include management of both choirs. She agreed, and I took the helm of the now-expanded role of Manager of Choral Activities.

My sails of confidence billowed under the leadership and mentorship of the choral activities program director, Dr. Charlene Archibeque, or "Dr. A," as we affectionately called her. Standing at a statuesque six feet tall, with Audrey Hepburn features, sophisticated attire, no-nonsense gait, and a voice that commanded authority, Dr. A's regal presence matched her reputation in the industry. In 1969, she had been the first woman ever to earn a Doctor of Musical Arts degree in choral conducting. In her career since then, she had conducted in many of the major music halls throughout the world, often as the first woman. She was (and as of this writing still is) recognized and sought-after by choral directors worldwide for her unique ability to transform ordinary choirs into extraordinary musical ensembles within just a few sessions.

Equally impressive as Dr. A's musical prowess was her business acumen. Her uncompromising drive to build audiences and to expose new ears to the beauty of truly inspired musical performance required running a tight ship of vocal, theatrical, operational, financial, marketing, and public relations excellence. Many of her students found her leadership style intimidating, and more than a few of them ended up at my desk in tears. Through it all, Dr. A's unrelenting pursuit of the exceptional made us all stronger musicians and stronger human beings, both individually and collectively. And she set the bar for me.

When I assumed the managerial helm in spring of 1991, the Concert Choir and Choraliers were planning a ten-day tour through southern California. The purpose of the tour was threefold: to recruit the best singers from the most talented high school and community college choirs by performing live concerts with them, to create bonding experiences for our own singers, and to gain exposure for SJSUs choirs in the broader music community. Dr. A had taken care of the "big rocks" by securing dates and venues for all of our performances, including one that would be broadcast on live television. Organizing the rest of the tour was up to me. I worked with our choral activities student leadership team, and together, we coordinated tour busses, accommodations, and schedules for 105 singers and staff.

Most days had two or three performances scheduled, but one of the middle days had only a single performance scheduled for the morning. The afternoon was slated for "free time" to give everyone's voice a rest. The more I thought about 105 college kids being turned loose in southern California for a whole afternoon and evening of "free time," the more I imagined all of the things that could go wrong with that. I envisioned the bus loaded up the next morning, running tight in our schedule to make the first performance of the day, and two or three of our singers being M.I.A. This was not a good scenario. I broached this topic with Dr. A in one of our weekly meetings in her office.

"Well," she said, "what are you going to do about it?"

At first, I thought her question was rhetorical. It wasn't.

"Me?" I inquired. I hadn't made the schedule. I didn't know any high school or community college choir directors. She was the one who had all of the connections. But wait — we weren't supposed to be singing, we were supposed to be resting our voices.

"There are two types of people in this world," Dr. A continued. "There are problem identifiers, and there are problem solvers. I hired you to be a problem solver. So, I'll ask you again, what are you going to do about that gap in the schedule?"

I paused a beat. Then the light bulb came on. "I'm going to fill it!" I replied with new found confidence.

"Good," she said. "Let me know what you need from me."

I loved this about Dr. A. She not only challenged me and gave me room to grow, but she also made it clear that she supported me in that growth.

The next day, I was back in Dr. A's office seeking approval to purchase a block of 105 tickets to the traveling Broadway production of *The Phantom of the Opera* at the Ahmanson Theater in Los Angeles with most of the original cast. The singers would love that. I had worked with the theater's box office, and we had managed to splice together a few sub-blocks of seats so that our singers could sit together. I had a forty-eight-hour hold on the seats.

"How do you propose to fund this purchase?" Dr. A challenged.

With that question, my education continued. I pulled together a group of student volunteers. We printed out a list of our most supportive donors and divvied it up between us, and we started calling. Within that forty-eight hours, we had secured the funding. I let Dr. A. know.

"Good," she said with a nod and a smile. That was all I needed. I bought the tickets.

When the rays of graduation finally shone above the horizon and illuminated what would have been my last semester at SJSU, my sails began to flutter in the winds of uncertainty. I wasn't ready for this season of my life to end. I had found an identity under Dr. A, but I had also derived my identity from my association with her. Who would I be on my own? The question was paralyzing. So much so that I dropped anchor and took an extension on my capstone research paper, making me ineligible to graduate, so that I could spend one more semester crewing for Dr. A. One more semester being who I was with Dr. A.

During that final, bonus semester of working and singing under Dr. A, I struck up a friendship with a fellow Choralier. Her name was Naomi, and I had met her on the European tour that had culminated in the Choir of the World competition. Naomi and I had gravitated toward one another as the only two people on that tour who had absolutely no complaints about the trip. While other singers were griping about the packed schedule, the small hotel rooms, the oddly-configured electrical outlets, the transparent toilet paper, the cramped bus, the unfamiliar food, and the fact that people whose first language was not English became annoyed when Americans expected them to understand English perfectly, Naomi and I were marveling at the countryside, the architecture, the history, the cultures, and the genuinely interesting people whom we encountered along the way.

Naomi was beautiful. She had a warmly pure soprano voice, big brown eyes, bright blonde curly hair, and an equally bright smile. She radiated pure joy and overflowed with an almost childlike exuberance for life. The light that she shined attracted everyone around her – audience members, friends, and an abundance of suitors. And me. I couldn't get enough of that light. I just had to be around her. And she seemed to see a light in me, too. We became fast friends, and we were inseparable during our last semester at SJSU. So much so that people stopped referring to us individually as Naomi or Tanya, they just called us "The Girls."

So, when the inevitable time came to leave the nest of Dr. A and the Choraliers behind, Naomi and I decided to keep the experience going, on our own. We formed a soprano duet. Kind of like the three tenors, only it was the two sopranos, *a cappella*. Naomi was the better singer, and I brought business chops to the partnership. We printed bright pink business cards: "Naomi & Tanya, Sopranos." Our business model was unique: We would arrive at private home dinner parties dressed in catering clothes, bringing with us all of the ingredients for a three-course Italian dinner. We would prepare the food in the host's kitchen, formally serve dinner and wine to the guests using the host's dining and stemware, and then duck into a bedroom to change clothes while everyone finished their meals. As the guests were enjoying dessert, we would reappear in long, black, sequined dresses and surprise and delight the host's guests by performing an intimate chamber music concert. People loved it! They would cry. They would get goosebumps. They would demand encore after encore. They would tip. Extremely well. And they would refer their friends.

Word got around fast, and within a few months of hatching our idea, we were booked nearly every day, sometimes twice in one day. We were also beginning to get handfuls of requests to perform outside of our local area. This sparked another idea: Maybe we could do a tour of our own. Maybe we could even tour Europe! One summer evening following a particularly successful performance, while sharing a glass of wine at a hilltop house where Naomi was house-sitting, we looked out over the sparkling lights of the Santa Clara valley and decided to just go for it. We would go to Europe the following summer, in 1993. We had one year to plan it out.

We were so excited, we could hardly contain ourselves. We had absolutely no idea how we were going to pull this off, but we were going on tour in Europe, and nothing was going to stop us! This night would forever be called "The Summit," and we would spend the rest of the night envisioning how we could do everything together, from then on. How we could make music together forever. Travel together. Stay in business together. How when we each got married, we could live in adjoining houses with a shared, common space. How our children could grow up and play together. How we wanted this moment of vision and hope, this Summit, to never end.

This was also the night that I fell in love with Naomi. I didn't tell her, and to this day, I don't think she ever knew. But my vision of our doing the rest of life together did not involve husbands, at least not in the way that hers did. Husbands could tag along as accessories, I supposed. Maybe be there somewhere in the background. Like extras in a movie. But the story that was unfolding in my imagination was a love story between Naomi and me, and in that moment, there was nothing that I wanted more.

As elated as I felt in that moment, this new feeling was also confusing for me. I had been raised in the Lutheran church as a Christian. My parents had dedicated my sister and me as babies. They had seen to it that we attended Sunday school and eighth grade confirmation classes where, after being baptized with a dribble of water on our foreheads and then handed a napkin, we publicly confirmed our Lutheran faith in front of the whole church, and then we took our first communion.

My Sunday school teachers had taught me what the Bible said about sex. With the opposite sex, it was wrong until after you were married. With the same sex, it was just plain wrong. I had had no problem with that. I had known just enough about anatomy to understand how the puzzle pieces were designed to fit, and that made sense to me. But what I was feeling for Naomi made no sense at all. Until I could figure it out, I would say nothing.

One of the things that I admired most about Naomi was her ability to believe for anything. No matter what she needed or set her mind to, she simply prayed, believed that the thing would come to pass, and then went right along with her life as if that thing had already happened. And the things happened! Needed funds would show up out of nowhere at the last minute. Lesser obligations would cancel whenever greater opportunities came along. One well-traveled supporter even gifted us with two open-ended, round-trip plane tickets to Europe – first class!

As we planned our tour, people would refer us to this relative or that contact who knew someone else who happened to have a place where we might be able to stay that was in or near a town where we hoped to perform. In the early 1990s, there was no internet and no email, so we *papier mâché-d* together an entire itinerary from scraps of paper that we had received at performances, international airmail that had taken weeks to deliver, and hand-written notes that we had jotted down during pay-by-the-minute long-distance phone conversations conducted in mashups of broken English, French, German, Spanish, Portuguese, and Italian. By the end of the year, we had a rough itinerary assembled, a pocket full of promised accommodations, and first-class airline reservations to Zurich, Switzerland, where we would be met by the Amstutz family, the first and most generous of our many gracious hosts.

During that year of preparation, I asked Naomi a lot of questions about believing, both what she believed and how she believed, and she shared a lot with me about her faith and about God. Naomi kept cassette tapes in her car with recordings of various ministers teaching the Word, and we would listen to them as we drove from house to house. These teachings didn't sound like the sermons that I had squirmed through on the hard, wooden church pews where I had sat with my parents on Sunday mornings growing up. The men and women whose voices spoke from these tapes read straight out of the Bible, explaining the meanings of the words and providing context of how each part fit into the bigger picture. They encouraged the listener to read and to study for themselves. They even encouraged the listener to ask questions and to pursue answers until they were satisfied that they had made the truth their own. These teachings were refreshingly non-religious, and I ate them up, especially as I grappled to reconcile my feelings for Naomi with what little that I had been taught about the Bible.

One afternoon, after listening to a tape recording of a teacher whose voice was now becoming familiar, Naomi sat me down for a serious talk. "There's something that we need to do," she said. I sat patiently as Naomi seemed to be mustering the courage to step into someplace painful. "There's this ministry that I used to be a part of. That's where all of these tapes came from. But some bad things happened, and I left. However, with all of these questions that you've been asking, there's a class that I know you need to take, and they have it."

The ministry that Naomi had been part of had fractured when the founding leader had died. As happens all too often with churches during times of leadership transition, politics had taken precedence above God, and the ministry that Naomi had called home had splintered into pieces, all under various leaders who thought that they should have been the anointed next-in-line. Naomi had left with one of the splinters. The remnant of the core group had retained the recorded teachings of the founder. Naomi had reached back out to the core group to get me into that class so that I could learn about the Word of God. We would be attending a home fellowship that evening.

CHAPTER SIX

The Fracture

The fellowship that Naomi and I attended was hosted by a delightful couple. They harbored no resentment against Naomi for her departure, and they welcomed us both with open arms, nurturing us weekly in faith and in fellowship, and shepherding me through the founder's recorded class. The seeds that were sown in my heart sprung up fast, and the light shone brighter in Naomi, too – so much so that in the months leading up to our departure for Europe, Naomi and I decided that upon our return, having no other plans to hold us back, we would enroll in ministry school and would dedicate the rest of our lives to serving God. Our year of preparation for a singing tour expanded to include preparation to share the Word along the way.

When our long-awaited departure date finally arrived, Naomi and I were full of anticipation and excitement. After a full day of flying that included entertaining our fellow passengers with a few of our favorite songs, we landed in Zurich, eager to share both our music and the Word of God with anyone who would listen. As we followed our dreams and our Eurail passes from country to country and from town to town, Naomi and I shared our faith as frequently as we shared our music, and more often than not, one would lead to the other.

While traveling through Sicily, Naomi and I had the pleasure of being invited to join a home fellowship that was affiliated with our ministry. We were greeted on that sunny, Sunday morning with a warm welcome by our host and with smiles, embraces, and kisses on alternate cheeks by a room crammed full of local Sicilians. Once everyone was seated, our host opened with prayer and then led the room in a session of robust singing and worship. And I do mean robust! With Sicilians, one hundred percent of all communication and expression involves their hands. In that small living room jam-packed full of people, it's a wonder that we all didn't get clobbered by the enthusiasm of the person next to us! After the teaching and a wonderful time of fellowship, our host sent us on our way with cannoli, pistachios, prayers, and well-wishes for a fruitful journey.

In addition to Sicily, Naomi's and my tour itinerary took us through Italy, Switzerland, Germany, Belgium, England, Wales, France, Spain, and Portugal. We were invited to sing for audiences large and small, performing in concert halls, cathedrals, banquet halls, churches, restaurants, and private homes. We were even made honorary citizens of the Tuscan town of Faenza after performing at a civic event for the town's leaders and prominent socialites. Throughout the tour, whenever the opportunity presented itself, we would step out and pray with people also.

Naomi and I were living our faith out loud, but internally, each of us was struggling with our own personal demons. As Naomi and I grew closer with each new day, I continued to grapple with the nature of my feelings for her. As much as I selfishly longed to tell her how I felt, and as much as I imagined a fictional world wherein she might quietly harbor similar feelings, I knew what the Bible said about sexuality, and I didn't know what to do with that. I was also really enjoying the closeness of my walk with God as well as my newfound fellowship with likeminded believers all over the world. Until I wrapped my head around what my heart was feeling, there was no way that I was going to risk losing everything, all over again, by doing something stupid.

As for Naomi, when she was in her late teens, she had found herself all but abandoned after her parents divorced. Consequently, the primary support system that she had had in the years before I met her had been her faith in God and her ministry family. I am convinced that these saved her life. I can only imagine how unsettling it must have been for her when the ministry fracture occurred. How betrayed and alone and vulnerable she must have felt. How much courage it must have required for her now to dare to try and trust the ministry or anyone again. I was adamant that I was not going to say or do anything that risked violating her trust or getting in the way of her walk with God. Whatever my feelings were, I loved her too much to strike at her faith. And so, I just went on loving Naomi with all of my heart, but I drew a clean line in the sand about how I expressed that love, and I never crossed it.

As summer turned to fall and Europeans returned to their home countries from their collective summer holidays, Naomi and I began to sense that the time had come for us, too, to return home. The experiences of our tour had been incredible, but we both knew that there was far more for us to learn and do. We took a final lap on our Eurail passes, simply as tourists, visiting bucket list sites that we had been too busy to squeeze in during the summer and reconnecting with a few dear friends that we had made along the way. Then, on a drizzly autumn morning, we bid the Amstutz family farewell, closed the book on an unforgettable tour, and boarded our first-class flight back home.

I cried the entire way from Zurich to San Francisco, completely overwhelmed with the emotions of turning the page from what had felt like the best years of my life and entering into a new and very different season. I knew that committing my life to God was the right decision for me, but it meant renouncing a life that had revolved around music after I had finally fully tasted how sweet such a life could be, and I was mourning that loss deeply. Also, while I had not physically expressed my feelings of sexuality with Naomi, I hadn't dealt with them either, I had simply stuffed them away. I knew that those feelings wouldn't stay buried forever, and I was fearful about when and how they might surface and what that would mean for the life that I intended to build now.

From the moment that I was safely back on the ground in California, my parents were thrilled to have me home. Their daughter had ventured out into the big, wide world for months on end and had survived on her own. She hadn't failed. She hadn't needed rescuing even once. She appeared to have returned none the worse for wear. All was right in the Simpson household.

My parents were less thrilled, however, with my plans to go to ministry school. This ministry was different from the church where I had grown up. My parents themselves had left the Lutheran church and now worshipped at the evangelical Christian church around the corner from my childhood home. But the ministry that I had gotten involved with was even more different than that. This ministry met in homes, not in a church building. There was no liturgy where everyone chanted the same call-and-response routine week after week. The elders didn't just get up and read from the Bible and then sit down, they taught us how to research the meaning ourselves. The preachers didn't speak quietly from a pulpit, they walked around and raised their voices with passion. Congregants didn't mumble rote prayers in unison, they overflowed with spirit-filled praise in words that were not written down and read from a page. Could it be that I was involved with some type of quasi-Christian church? Was this ministry really Christian at all? Was their daughter in danger? Did she need saving?

To quell my parents' concerns, I invited them to attend a Sunday morning home fellowship with me. To sweeten the invitation, I had chosen a Sunday when Naomi and I would be singing a song that I myself had arranged. I was sure that once my parents experienced the fellowship for themselves, their fears would be assuaged. Heck, they might even enjoy it. My parents took me up on my offer, and that Sunday morning, they accompanied me to the home of the wonderful leadership couple who had been so instrumental in developing my faith. So many people showed up that day that we had to move the whole operation from the couple's living room out into their backyard in order for everyone to fit. The message was great that morning.

Naomi's and my song went beautifully and was well-received. The fellowship was sweet, and everyone there enjoyed meeting and talking with my parents.

My parents, however, did not enjoy the experience at all. Why were we at a home instead of in a church building? Why were we outdoors? Why didn't we all recite the same prayers at the same time? Why did the minister have to shout so loud? My parents came away from the experience even more concerned than they had been before.

I was undeterred. My parents' reaction to my choice of ministry was not unlike their reaction to modern music, or to modern fashion, or to modern anything, for that matter. It was just different from what they were used to. I was sure that they would come around.

Shortly after returning to California, as part of our preparation to enter ministry school, Naomi and I each were assigned to different towns to apprentice under the mentorship of local leaders for a season of learning and growing and teaching and reaching out within our respective communities. Naomi was assigned to the same town as our current leadership couple, and I was assigned over the hill to the town of Capitola. Naomi was admitted to enroll in ministry school the following summer; however, I was younger in my spiritual development, so my admission was delayed to allow more time for me to grow in faith prior to enrollment. This was a difficult message for both Naomi and me to hear, as we had hoped to matriculate through the three-year program together. But we pushed forward, deferring to the wisdom of our ministry leaders as the Bible instructed us to do.

The year that Naomi enrolled in ministry school, I was reassigned to San Diego, California. With gracious support from local believers, I thrived in my newly assigned town. I had the opportunity to learn from knowledgeable teachers, build and lead a home fellowship in my own apartment, and even write and sing music with fellow believers and perform those songs at the state level. Naomi wrote to me from ministry school, sharing her experiences there and inspiring me with the many things that she was learning. This season was shaping up to be all of the things that I had hoped for and none of the things that I had feared.

And then, out of nowhere, it all came crashing down.

The first cracks appeared when my local ministry leader called me to impart some difficult news. Ministry headquarters had instructed him to inform me that Naomi and I were not to speak to each other or to communicate with one another directly in any way. When we happened to see each other at gatherings or events, we would be permitted to exchange a simple greeting, but that would be all. No reason was given.

This message was both heartbreaking and extremely confusing. What could possibly have happened? Why on earth would a ministry forbid fellow believers from communicating with one another? And why Naomi and me? It didn't make any sense to me. However, as stunned as I was, it was clear that I had no say in the matter. I knew that failure to comply with the instruction would surely mean the end of any future enrollment in ministry school for me at best, and I didn't even dare to imagine anything worse. I just couldn't risk losing everything again. And so, in my disciplined commitment to follow Biblical protocol and submit to ministry leadership, I complied with the instruction, continuing to trust the wisdom of my leaders.

A few months later, a senior leader at ministry headquarters requested a phone call with me, which was highly unusual. Something had happened at the school, and they had questions for me pertaining to Naomi. I didn't know what had happened at the school or why leadership needed to hear from me, and the questions that the senior leader asked me shed no light on the matter. However, apparently my answers were not what he was expecting to hear. The next thing that I knew, Naomi was no longer enrolled in the school.

I was devastated. In answering that senior leader's questions, I had betrayed Naomi's trust, disclosing private information that was not mine to share. Betraying Naomi's trust was the one thing that I had vowed never to do, under any circumstance. Yet when I had been instructed by that senior leader to break that vow and to disclose information that Naomi had shared with me in confidence, I had obeyed the instruction without hesitation and without question. That obedience didn't feel Godly, it felt foul.

More cracks appeared when I received another call from my local ministry leader, this time instructing me not to contact the leadership couple in my hometown who had taken such good care of Naomi and me since the time that we had first attended fellowship in their home. I agreed without question, but I began to get an uncomfortable feeling that something was very wrong.

A few weeks later, I traveled to my hometown for a quick weekend visit with my parents. Upon my arrival there, I was again contacted by leadership and was firmly admonished not to communicate with that couple. I found this second admonishment oddly unnecessary and also hurtful. Did my leaders not trust that I would comply with their original instruction? Had I not followed every single instruction that they had given me thus far, without question? Had I given them any reason not to trust me?

I was further directed to attend a specific home fellowship that weekend with a newly-assigned and unfamiliar leader. I hadn't planned to attend any home fellowship that weekend. I had wanted to make the most of the limited time that I had in town to spend with my parents. However, given the tenor of the conversation, I did as I was told, but I was getting an even more uncomfortable sense that something was seriously off.

The final cracks that blew everything apart for me appeared when my assigned ministry leader called me to come to his home, along with a single mom who had been faithfully attending my home fellowship and her teenage daughter who had not been attending. After exchanging a few niceties, this leader suddenly uncoiled and launched into a diatribe of vitriol, yelling and screaming at the teenage girl and calling her unspeakable names because she would not come to my home fellowship meetings with her mother. This screaming went on for hours. The meeting ended with the leader kicking the sobbing mother out of the ministry for not being spiritually strong enough to control her teenage daughter.

I left that meeting stunned. I didn't know how to process what I had just witnessed. How could I have just sat there and said nothing while this man yelled at this poor girl for hours while her mother wept? Something was horribly wrong. I went home and made a few phone calls and was sickened to discover that the reason that I had been instructed not to contact the wonderful leadership couple in my hometown was because the ministry had ripped that family apart, banishing the husband for reasons unknown and instructing the wife to take their four children and to leave her husband if she wanted to stay in the ministry. I couldn't believe it. These were wonderful believers who loved God, were committed to the ministry, and were fiercely devoted to one another. Politics had not been eradicated from the ministry after the fracture. They had grown worse and more ugly.

That night, I went through my entire apartment and gathered up every item in my possession that belonged to the ministry or to anyone in it. I put all of it into a bag along with a note, drove the bag to my leaders' house, and dropped it on their front doorstep. And then, I walked away. From those leaders, from the ministry, from everyone I knew (including Naomi, whom I knew would be forbidden to contact me), and from God.

CHAPTER SEVEN

Un-Christian

The morning after I walked away from the ministry, I woke up in my apartment feeling very disoriented. Like when you wake up in a hotel room in the dark, and for a minute, you don't know where you are. Except that the more I tried to get my bearings, the more I realized that I didn't have any. Everything that I knew and loved was gone. Music was gone. Naomi was gone. My budding life in ministry was gone. My sense of self was gone. My trust in everyone around me was gone. My faith in God was gone. I lay in my bed, paralyzed. I didn't know what to do. I certainly wasn't going to call my parents and endure another round of pity and "I told you so." I allowed myself the grace to succumb to my feelings of despair, and I sobbed deeply.

"Alright, that's enough," I eventually shook myself as I wiped away tears. "I may not know what I'm supposed to do now, but lying in bed all day surely isn't it." I sat up, put my feet on the ground, took several deep breaths, then took stock of what, if anything, I had left, figuratively wiggling my fingers and toes after my car accident all over again. I searched the empty inventory of my self-worth and spotted one small item remaining on a shelf, way in the back: I had a job. It was just an ordinary job doing ordinary clerical work in an ordinary company, but it was something. And something was better than nothing.

So, I did the only thing that I knew to do. I got myself up out of bed, I got ready for work, I got into my car, and I went to my job. At the end of the work day, I got back into my car, and I went back home to my apartment. And then, the next day, I did all of that again. And then again. In between, I bought groceries, I paid my bills, I washed my laundry, and I did all of the sorts of things that people do. I just kept going through the motions, numb, for months. But I kept going.

In the years since I walked away, I've often pondered why I walked away from God. Why didn't I just walk away from those leaders, or from that ministry? Why did I give God the black eye? Life sure would have gotten a whole lot better a whole lot sooner if I had drawn closer to God in that moment instead of pushing Him away.

I think part of the reason is that I was ashamed. The ministry that I had been part of had had a reputation for being a cult. I didn't believe then, and looking back with clear eyes, I don't believe now that it was a cult. "Cult" is a term that has been tossed around far too loosely by mainstream religions who are averse to understanding or accepting ways of worship that are different from their own. In the late twentieth century, mainstream Christianity, in particular, found it easier to ostracize those who worshipped in non-traditional settings or in non-traditional ways than it was to admit that maybe, just maybe, there might be something to be gained by pulling together as a Christian body, rather than digging in with heels of factionalism.

But during the time I was involved with the ministry, many around me looked down upon my budding Christianity. My parents were certain that I had lost my way. My music friends wrote me off as having gotten wrapped up in something nefarious. It seemed like everyone that I knew was adamant that they were right, and I was wrong, and therefore all of my beliefs were somehow invalid. Un-Christian. So, when things went sour with the ministry, when what I really needed was wise counsel, all I heard was an endless chorus of "I told you so."

Another part of the reason that I walked away from God is that while I rightly expected perfection from God, I wrongly extended that same expectation of perfection to church leaders. I didn't leave any room for human fallibility in my ministry leaders, so when they acted imperfectly, I attributed that imperfection to God. Granted, some of the stuff that I experienced in the ministry was bad. Really, really bad. But those were the actions of people.[4] Regardless of whether I dealt with the people by slogging through the muck with them until they found their way or by walking away from them, my real failure was to impugn the integrity of God based upon my disappointment in people.

I think, though, that the best explanation for why I walked away from God is that the seed of the Word that had been sown in me had fallen on shallow, rocky ground. I was too new in my walk with God, and the soil of my heart had not been sufficiently prepared for the Word to take root. When the cracks that appeared in the ministry collided with the echoes of "cult" that I was hearing all around me, I just didn't have enough root to hold on to God through the storm, and I fell away.

───────────

My apartment and workplace at that time were both located just south of San Diego, California, in neighboring towns within a few miles of each other. The company that I worked for was a graphic and interior design-build operation specializing in signs and sales center interiors for new home developments, primarily in the western part of the country. When I had been assigned by the ministry to start and grow a home fellowship in the town of Chula Vista where I now lived, I had also taken on a clerical job at this company in nearby National City.

───────────

4   From what I hear, the ministry did some housekeeping shortly after I left, and today it is a healed household with many strong believers.

My job was an administrative assistant role that directly supported the president of the company.

The president's name was Bob, and Bob was a true entrepreneur. Upon being discharged from the marines after serving honorably in combat in Vietnam, Bob employed his younger brother, Tony, and with help from their dear friend and mentor, Dave, they cobbled together a small business, painting and posting weekend directional signs along roadway shoulders to drive prospective home buyer traffic to new housing developments. The company started out as a small, scrappy operation run out of Bob's garage, but Bob was a born salesman, Dave was a gifted businessman, and Tony was the hardest working guy that I had ever met. By the time I joined the company, they were celebrating twenty years in business, and the company had divisional locations throughout the western United States and a large, consolidated manufacturing and shipping facility at their corporate headquarters where I worked.

Bob reminded me of Dr. A in many ways. His drive for both growth and uncompromised excellence was intimidating to some, but he had a big heart for supporting and developing internal talent and for making a positive impact on the communities in which his company did business. My desk was situated right outside of Bob's office, so I had the benefit of observing the comings and goings of various company leaders and external partners and overhearing bits and pieces of strategic conversations. I quickly ascertained that Bob was someone from whom I could learn much, and I was determined to rebuild my sense of self-worth by working more closely with him and by contributing to the company in a bigger way.

Directly across from my desk, in the office next to Bob's, sat the director of marketing. I would watch her day after day, coming and going from this event and that, always flustered and in a hurry and overflowing with armfuls of pictures and color swatches and presentation materials and outfits for her various events. It was hard to tell exactly what she did, but it seemed to me that despite all of that busy-ness, it really didn't look all that difficult, and I couldn't figure out why she seemed so stressed out all the time. I was intrigued.

One afternoon, after spending most of the day working up my nerve, I mustered the courage to knock on her door and ask her if she had a minute. "Not really," she said, "but if you help me carry these things to my car, we can talk on the way out." As we hurried out to her car, I told her that I was fascinated by what she did and was eager to learn more about her work, and I offered to help her out whenever I had down time. She didn't think that she would have much time in her schedule to teach me anything, but she was grateful for my offer of help, and she took me up on that. As she entrusted me with tasks of gradually increasing responsibility, I was soon assembling her presentation materials and writing marketing copy for award submissions and press releases. I loved the creative aspect of the work, and I had been right: it really wasn't all that difficult.

Several months later, as I was wrapping up the end of an ordinary work day, the marketing director slunk out of Bob's office, visibly distraught. When I arrived at work the following morning, her office was empty. I didn't know what had happened, but I was much more interested in the opportunity that this situation represented than I was in what might have caused it. I spent that whole day and all night that night assembling a presentation of my own. The next morning, it was Bob's office door that I was knocking on. "Do you have a minute?" I asked. "Not really," he said, "but I have some time this afternoon. You can come back then."

That afternoon, I found myself sitting across from Bob at the small conference table in his office, pitching him a presentation and spinning my best argument about why I was the perfect person to fill the vacant role of marketing director. Never mind that I had no marketing education and had never done anything more than help assemble presentation materials and write a bit of copy. I could do it! I just knew I could! All I needed was a chance.

Bob laughed. Heartily. I stayed put. I just kept looking at him, right in the eyes.

"You're serious, aren't you," he finally said. Just like the managing broker at the stock brokerage had said to me so many years ago.

"I can do this," I said.

"Well, let me think about it," he said.

My heart was silently bursting with hope. I did my very best to keep a solemn face, although I'm sure that a hint of a smile must have found its way to the corners of my lips. I had learned enough about sales from my days at the brokerage and from watching and listening to Bob to know that – if you were really good at selling – any answer that wasn't a hard no could be turned into a yes. Bob hadn't said no! I was over the moon.

The next day, I arrived at work early. I anxiously plugged away at menial tasks while the usual parade of people came and went from Bob's office all morning. When Bob finally emerged from his morning meetings, he told me that he was headed out to lunch, and then he left. Not a word about our conversation the day before. I didn't budge, I sat right there and ate lunch at my desk. I wasn't moving from that seat until I could catch Bob on his way back in from lunch. About an hour later, Bob returned from lunch, walked straight into his office, and closed the door. *Now what do I do?*

The parade of afternoon meetings came and went. Finally, at the end of the day, Bob stuck his head out the door. "Come in for a minute," he said. I could tell from the sound of Bob's voice that this wasn't going to be the conversation that I had hoped for. "Close the door," he said before I could sit down. Ugh. This was not going to be what I had hoped for at all. "I've given your proposal some thought," Bob said, "and I just can't make you marketing director."

My heart fell. I had gotten my hopes up too high. I should have known better. Somebody like me didn't deserve that job. I didn't know anything about marketing. I didn't know anything about anything. I should just be grateful to have the job that I had. I should be grateful to have a job at all. But oh, how I had wanted that marketing director job! It would have made me somebody. A clerical worker was nobody, but a marketing director was somebody.

"However," Bob continued, "here's what we can do…"

I will forever be grateful for what Bob said next. He was willing to give me a shot, but with lesser responsibility until I earned a marketing degree. I had three years to get that done. In the meantime, it was up to me to seek out Dave and Tony and the divisional leaders to learn the company's products, customers and market. Then, if all was still going well when I got my degree, the marketing job would be mine. I couldn't believe my ears! I jumped at the chance. I told Bob that I was willing to do the work to get the degree, but that I had no way to pay for it.

"You just find a legitimate academic program and get yourself admitted," he said. "We can work out the tuition."

I jumped right on it and enrolled in the University of San Diego's school of business before Bob could change his mind. After two years of working my tail off to learn the company by day and taking a full-time load of courses by night, I graduated with an MBA from USD in 1999 with a triple concentration in marketing, finance, and entrepreneurship. And, true to his promise, Bob promoted me – to vice president of marketing. Now, that was somebody!

CHAPTER EIGHT

Lake Pillsbury

I enjoyed my role in marketing. I got to work around creative types nearly all of the time, and working in the building industry, especially around Bob and Tony and Dave, reminded me of some of the fonder memories of my childhood. My dad was an architectural engineer, Dad's older brother – my Uncle Dick – was a construction genius, their father – my grandfather – was a finish carpenter, and my mother had minored in interior design. Between all of them, there was always some type of project going on around our house, whether it was installing shelves, building cabinetry, or rearranging the living room furniture for the umpteenth time.

When I was a toddler, Uncle Dick came into possession of a very steep parcel of land that abutted the shore of Lake Pillsbury, a remote, off-grid lake in northern California. Because of the steepness of the terrain, the parcel was considered unbuildable and of minimal value. Enter my father, the architectural engineer. All you had to do was tell Dad that something couldn't be done, and he would find a way to do it. Dad designed a cluster of small, stilted, A-frame buildings connected by outdoor stairways that, taken together, comprised a wonderfully livable summer vacation set-up for two families.

Every summer Friday afternoon, Mom and Dad would load a giant cooler, several boxes of food, a few suitcases, our black Labrador Retriever, Joaquín (Dad finally was allowed to name somebody

Joaquín!), and my sister and me into our Griswold-style Ford Country Squire station wagon with fake wood paneling and green vinyl seats, and we would drive the five hours from San José to Lake Pillsbury. The drive was typically spent with Mom and Dad trying to listen to a San Francisco Giants baseball game on the radio, my sister singing at the top of her lungs out of her rolled-down window, and me doing my best to torment my sister until she would get in trouble for taking the bait.

From the day that Uncle Dick acquired that property until to the day that our families eventually sold it, that place was continuously under construction. Neither my family nor Uncle Dick's family ever seemed to have very much money, but Dad, Uncle Dick, and Grandpa had amazing skills. Between the three of them, Uncle Dick's four boys, and some occasional help and "supervision" from the neighbors, they put their minds and backs into the job and built that place themselves. To this day, I can't smell saw dust without being taken right back to childhood summers at Lake Pillsbury.

Every Saturday morning at seven a.m. sharp, my mother, my sister and I, and every neighbor at our end of the lake, would awaken to the sound of chain saws or table saws or hammers pounding away. My mother and aunt had insisted that their husbands were not to make noise any earlier than seven, and five-o-clock meant that it was time for them to put down their tools and get cleaned up for happy hour. On the occasional Saturday afternoon, if the wind was just right, we would look up and see Dad headed down the path to the lake early with a bag of sails in hand. He would rig up his Hobie Cat, grab Mom, and the two of them would set off zipping across the lake. Dad lived for those afternoons of sailing with Mom. If his smile had been any wider, the corners of his mouth might have wrapped around his ears permanently.

On Saturday afternoons, Lake Pillsbury bustled with activity. Up and down the shoreline, men sat in beach chairs drinking beer, women reclined in chaise lounges reading Harlequin romance novels, children splashed and squealed in the water, and teenage girls lay on display as far out on the docks as they could get, applying suntan oil and sizing up the teenage boys who would parade back and forth on water skis or on stand-up Jet Skis, occasionally "accidentally" dousing a girl that they liked with a rooster tail of lake water.

Saturday evenings were spent together with neighbors, often on a flotilla of lashed-together pontoon boats in the middle of the lake, with beverage coolers of Salty Dogs and free-flowing Manhattans lubricating stories and jokes that would grow more colorful as the evening progressed. But Sunday mornings at seven a.m. sharp, the construction would begin again and would progress until noon, at which point Dad and Uncle Dick would put all of their tools away, everyone would have lunch, and then our family would load up the car and retrace the same five-hour drive in reverse.

Some weeks, Mom, my sister, Joaquín, and I would all stay at the lake while Dad drove back and forth to San José for work. During the week, Lake Pillsbury was quiet. This was my favorite time. I would sit out on the empty dock reading books, composing songs, writing in a journal, or simply staring up at the sky, taking in the shapes of the clouds and being in awe of the wonder of this tiny planet that we live on and everything that had to come together just right so that we all could be here to enjoy it.

Lake Pillsbury was a special place for me, a place that I came back to whenever I needed to clear my head, even as an adult. It was here that I had sat alone on the edge of the dock after I left the ministry, tearing the pages out of my journal from that time, one by one, immersing them beneath the surface of the water until all of the ink washed away. Symbolically erasing my unaddressed emotions about Naomi and my unfinished business with God.

In my new role at work, one of the products that I was responsible for marketing was three-dimensional, electronic, architectural renderings. These fascinated me. They were computerized creations that brought to life the kinds of drawings that I had seen on my father's drafting board growing up. As I was coming up to speed in my role, I was excited to meet with the manager of electronic renderings. I had set up a time to tour his studio to learn how those animated versions of buildings were brought to life. A few days before that scheduled meeting, a man popped his head into my office on his way by to see Bob.

"Hi, I'm Paul," he said with a smile. "I just wanted to introduce myself. We'll be meeting in my studio on Friday."

This man was handsome! He looked nothing like the teddy-bear-shaped "husband material" that I had married the first time. This man was fit and lean like my father, and something about his peppy, cheerful demeanor and crooked smile set off sparks in me. With just a simple greeting, I had something to look forward to on Friday that was even more interesting than computerized architectural renderings.

Paul and I hit it off from day one. Paul was smart, fun, witty, kind, and full of life. He was a gentleman and a gentle man. He played guitar and loved all kinds of music, including the big band jazz that I had played on trombone and even the classical choral music that I had sung. He loved animals. He loved boating. And best of all, he loved me.

Paul and I took things slow. Paul was just coming out of a divorce that he hadn't wanted, and I was just coming out of the ministry fiasco. We both had a lot of healing to do. But the pull of the magnet could not be denied, and four years later, with my parents' enthusiastic blessing, Paul and I were married.

As the twentieth century gave way to the early 2000s, I was living the modern American dream. I was a rising-star executive making more money than I had ever imagined that I would. I had met and married a wonderful husband who loved me dearly. We lived in a perfectly manicured master-planned community in a large four-bedroom, three-bathroom McMansion with two dogs in the yard and two cars and an SUV parked in our three-car garage. We enjoyed evenings relaxing with cocktails in our hot tub that was nestled between palms in a corner of our landscaped backyard, and we spent weekends boating with friends on the San Diego Bay. The only thing missing from this idyllic picture was children, and we had stopped actively preventing those, so it was just a matter of time before our little family of two humans and two dogs would be growing. By all worldly standards, I should have been blissfully happy. Instead, I felt unsettled, both in my job and in my marriage.

Two things that came as part and parcel of a career in marketing were lots of networking events and lots of industry conferences. Nearly every industry event had a hosted bar, and when the hosts' tabs closed, there was no shortage of businessmen who were eager to step up and keep the libations flowing, and who made no secret of their hopes that their generosity would be reciprocated in the form of extracurricular activity. This environment was nauseatingly reminiscent of my experience at the brokerage. However, pretending to be grateful for unwelcome affection was the required price of acceptance into this male-dominated networking crowd, so I gritted my teeth, fended off the worst of the ogling and pawing, and did my best to retain my integrity, sometimes with greater success than others.

There was quite a bit of drinking happening at home, too. Paul and I had met at a time when he was rebounding from a failed marriage, and I was rebounding from the ministry disaster and from my loss of music. Neither Paul nor I had taken enough time to process those losses on our own. We were two broken people who had found refuge and comfort in each other's arms, but who hadn't let each other into the intimate, vulnerable places in our hearts. Diving into the messy parts of each other's hopes and fears and dreams and regrets would have meant risking the safe harbor of the marriage that we had created. We had both been hurt deeply, and we had now traded away the perils of deep connection for a marriage that was comfortable on a nice, easy, surface level.

I did make one attempt to venture into deeper waters with Paul. I had been keeping a journal around the time that Paul and I had met, and I had filled it with all of the happiness and excitement and giddiness that surrounds new love. I had written poetry as well as detailed accounts of all of my most intimate thoughts about Paul and about my growing love for him. My journals were never meant to be shared with anyone, but for Paul, I had decided to take an emotional risk and make an exception. I wanted my husband to know me. I nervously wrapped up my journal in hand-made paper, took a deep breath, and presented it to Paul on his birthday.

When Paul opened my gift, he didn't know what it was at first. I explained the journal to him, the time period that it had come from, what it contained, and what it meant for me to share it with him. Paul's reaction surprised me. He could not have handed that journal back to me faster if it had been radioactive. He didn't want it. It was too personal. I blinked with confusion and attempted to explain again, but it was no use. My emotional risk had backfired. Paul did not want to read that journal.

Paul's rejection of my journal felt like a rejection of me. Like the surface me was loveable, but the deep, real me was not. Like everyone would be better off if the deep, real me simply didn't exist. Looking back now, I'm sure that Paul's rejection of my journal was more about his own inability to be vulnerable at that point in his life than it was about anything to do with me, but it hit me hard all the same.

From that moment on, Paul and I kept our conversation light, lived our relationship on the surface, and drank a lot. Weekday evenings at home would typically include dinner and several martinis, after which we would settle in to watch whatever was on TV that night. On one of those nights, Paul had passed out on the couch before the end of the first show, and I was in not much better shape. I stumbled into the bathroom, and when I looked in the mirror, I didn't recognize the bleary-eyed image looking back at me. Where was the little girl who had been so full of hopes and dreams and music and life? Where was the young woman who had just wanted to live her life for God? Even after all of my failures, God had given me a second chance at a good job and a good husband who loved me, but how could I be a good wife and take care of Paul and us – and potentially children – when I didn't even know how to take care of myself? Instead of moving forward, I was headed back toward the self that I had run away from when I had left the brokerage.

I broke down hard. I could not be this shallow, surface self anymore. I needed help – real help, the kind that helps you change, not the kind that rescues you and deposits you right back where you were before. I didn't know who to turn to. I wasn't speaking to God. I couldn't talk to my husband. My sister and I weren't close. And in all my life, my parents and I had never had any deep conversations. They had always been there to swoop in to save me and to provide guidance and direction. But whenever I brought up anything uncomfortable that conflicted with their point of view, either the discussion would shut down entirely or it would pivot from a conversation to one-way instruction. They imparted the instruction, and I was to follow it. "Children, obey your parents in the Lord: for this is right," the Bible said. I drug my inebriated self and my blacked-out husband upstairs to bed that night, feeling utterly alone, and I cried myself to sleep.

As I was getting ready for work that next morning, I knew that something had to change. I had to try to talk with my parents. I was ready to run. I had already drafted a Dear John letter to Paul, but it didn't feel right. I needed someone to talk me out of it in a way that I could hear. I didn't need my parents to just tell me what to do and then shut down. I needed someone who would listen without judging, someone who would try to understand, someone who would help me to formulate a plan, someone who would walk through the messiness with me. Only then would I be able hear what I really hoped that they would say: Get back in there! Keep going! Don't give up! We believe in you!

Maybe now that I was married and had a career, my parents would talk with me adult-to-adult. Maybe I could try to talk with one of them. Maybe this time would be different. I swallowed hard, picked up the phone, and called my father. I asked him if we could go together to Lake Pillsbury that weekend. I had some thinking to do, and I could use his wisdom. Dad agreed. I flew to San José that Friday, and we drove to the lake together.

During the whole, five-hour ride to Lake Pillsbury, Dad and I chatted about nothing in particular. Baseball. Work. How Mom was doing. How my sister was doing. What project Dad was going to work on at the lake that weekend. Anything but what I really needed to talk about. Saturday went by. Sunday went by. We would be leaving on Monday. As Dad and I sat out on the deck that Sunday evening, watching the shadows grow while the sun set over the mountain behind us, I broached the topic.

"Dad, Paul and I are having some trouble."

Dad knew that the lake was where I came to think. Where I came to wrestle with big issues. We hadn't talked about it, but he knew. He also knew that I had come to the lake right before Luke and I had divorced. Dad was clearly uncomfortable with where this seemed to be headed. He loved Paul like the son that he had never had, and this was just too much for him.

"I can't have this conversation," Dad choked.

I was heartbroken. I'm not sure what I had expected Dad to say. I didn't even care if he said anything. I had just needed him to listen. Throughout my whole life, no matter what had happened, I could always count on Dad to be there for me. Dad always came through. Like gravity – you don't question it. Yet with those few words, gravity had come out from underneath me.

Dad and I sat quietly on the deck together while all of the light drained out of the sky. We went to bed without saying a word. The next day, we drove back to San José in silence. Dad dropped me off at the airport with a sad hug, and I flew home.

CHAPTER NINE

The Runner

When I walked in the front door of my home in San Diego, Paul was waiting for me with red, tear-soaked eyes. He had read the Dear John letter that I had left on the bathroom counter where I knew that he would find it. He didn't understand. Of course he didn't. How could he? Even I didn't understand. Through tears of my own, I told him what I knew: I didn't know who I was, and I needed some space to figure that out. I went upstairs to collect a few things to wear for the next several days. I would come back for the rest.

Paul waited for me at the bottom of the stairs. As I descended the steps with my arms full of clothes, I collapsed on a landing midway down and bawled.

"Please don't go," Paul pleaded.

"I have to," I cried with more certainty than I felt. I silently wished that Paul would say something to convince me to stay. Some magic words that could break through this fog of confusion and make me believe that I mattered to him. Not just our marriage, but me. Something that said not just "I love you," but "I see you."

Neither of us said anything. Neither of us knew how. I stood up and made my way down the rest of the steps to the door. We stood at the door for an extended moment looking into each other's eyes, Paul with his hand on the doorknob, each of us hoping that the other would say something. Each of us hoping that the other could fix this somehow. Neither of us could. After a long silence, Paul turned the knob and opened the door.

"I love you," Paul wept as he held the door open for me.

"I love you, too," I sobbed. And then I walked out the door.

I drove to a short-term rental as a place to try to clear my head, but as the days turned into weeks, my mind simply spun. Working in the same company with Paul, I felt like all of my disillusionment with the ways of the business world and all of my despair over my marriage were closing in on me at once. I was too immersed in everything that was wrong to be able to see or to think. To be able to shake off the self that I could no longer stand be.

And so, I did what I had always done when I didn't like who I had become: I packed up my life and I ran. Just like I had run away from the brokerage and from the ministry. I quit my job, I filed for divorce, and I ran. Away from my husband. Away from my home. Away from my marketing career. And I ran away from myself.

When I ran away from everything, I ran all the way to Panama City, Florida, and I landed at the home of a dear friend. His name was Tevye, and Tevye had been a highly accomplished, semi-famous traveling musician in the seventies. Tevye lived alone in a large, waterfront home on a bayou, and he had a guest room available where he said that I was welcome to stay as long as I needed.

Tevye worked outside of the house during the daytime and often into the evening, leaving me lots of quiet time to sit alone, look out over the bayou, and think. When Tevye was at home, he would regale me with tale upon tale of his musical adventures. Occasionally, if I was particularly lucky and he wasn't too tired, he would pick up one of his many guitars and sing me a song or two. These were precious times, and they were a much needed coming-up-for-air from my hours of thinking.

Even more than his stories and his songs, the thing that I appreciated most about Tevye was his ability to listen. Tevye was twenty-five years older than I was, but rather than lecturing me as a father would a child, he listened to me as a friend, without judgement, without instruction, and without attempting to rescue me. He just listened intently, offering well-timed, provocative questions and comments to nudge me to dig a little bit deeper. For the first time in a long time, I felt seen.

One day, Tevye was showing me a set of plans that he had drawn up years earlier to convert a very large section of his home into his dream kitchen and living area. Tevye beamed with pride as he walked me virtually through every aspect of the drawings. I thought that his plans looked fantastic, and I asked him why he hadn't done the conversion all of those years ago, and if he was considering doing it now. Tevye's face dropped. That section of his home was stuffed from wall to wall and floor to ceiling with stacks of boxes and piles of treasures. The mere thought of dealing with all of the items stored in that part of his home was enough to send him spiraling into overwhelm.

"How long has all of that stuff been sitting there?" I asked.

"Years."

"Do you even know what all is in there?"

"Well, some of it yes, but a lot of it, no."

"How much use and enjoyment are you getting out of all of those things now?"

"Obviously none. It's actually making me depressed looking at all of that every day."

"Hmmm... The way I see it," I started, "is that you have three options. One is to do nothing. If you do nothing, all of that stuff will sit right there until after you die, and then your children will have to go through it. In the meantime, you'll be depressed looking at all of it piled up there, and you'll never get to enjoy any of it or to do anything with that space."

Tevye looked disheartened. He said nothing.

I continued. "The second option is to throw every single thing in that room away. Take it all to the dump! You'll get the same amount of use and enjoyment out of all of that stuff that you're getting now, which is zero, but you won't be depressed looking at it, and you can build your dream kitchen."

Tevye was horrified. "I can't just throw everything away! I need those things! There are memories in there!"

"Okay, okay! Hold on. There is a third option." I squared up and made my case. "The third option is that we go through all of it together. Or you go through it with somebody that you hire, if you don't want me looking through your things. If somebody helps you, then they can keep you from getting stuck in overwhelm while you go through it. Once that's done, then you will be able to enjoy all of your things, you won't be depressed looking at all of that mess, *and* you can build your dream kitchen!"

Tevye shook his head. "No, nobody else can help me with that stuff. I have to go through everything myself, because I have to make decisions about each item. I'll just do it myself, a little bit at a time."

"How realistic do you think that is, that it will ever get done that way?"

"It isn't," Tevye conceded.

"On this, we agree," I said. "So, if going through all of this on your own isn't a real option, and if you won't let anyone help you either, then what you're really saying is that you're choosing option one, which is to do nothing."

Tevye was quiet.

"If you're going to do option one," I concluded, "then you might as well do option two and take everything to the dump. Either way, you'll never see any of your things again, but at least you won't have to be depressed looking at all of those piles!"

"Agh, stop!" Tevye exclaimed. "You argue like a lawyer!"

Our conversation turned to other things for the rest of the evening. Nevertheless, as I was thinking about the discussion later that night, I realized that this was not the first (nor would it be the last) time that someone had told me that I argued like a lawyer. But something in the way that Tevye had said it sparked a thought: maybe that's something that I could do. Maybe I could be lawyer. Maybe I could channel my passion for rhetoric into something that would give me a clean start.

And that was it. The seed was planted. With much the same ignorance that I had walked into Room 150 at SJSU, I charged blindly into a grand new venture that would be sufficiently mind-consuming to override the crisis at hand. As I had done both with the brokerage and with my marketing career, I ran from my emotions and my unaddressed questions of identity by stuffing them into a tightly-sealed box and shoving that box to the back of my mental closet to deal with "later," subconsciously plotting that if I played my cards right, "later" may never have to come.

I set right to work turning myself into a lawyer. I signed myself up to take the LSAT, figured out which law school was closest to where I lived, and filled out an application for admission to Florida State University. As far as I knew, other than maybe Harvard or Yale, a law school was a law school, and if you wanted to go, you filled out a form, you took a test, you wrote a check, and you showed up. I didn't know that the LSAT was hard. I didn't know that getting into law school was hard. I didn't know that FSU was a top tier law school. If I had known any of these things, I probably would have dismissed the whole idea as the lark that it was and moved on to pursue something else instead. But, as had been my nature, not a lot of aiming happened between "ready" and "fire." I just pulled the trigger and went for it and would figure it out along the way.

One spring afternoon, several months after having taken the LSAT and achieving a respectable score, I was going through the day's stack of mail, and I pulled out an envelope from FSU. By that time, I had done a bit more homework. Law school was going to be a three-year-long, full-time, live-on-site kind of an undertaking. It was going to require reading hundreds of pages per night, memorizing the main points of all of those pages, and remembering both the gist and the source of those main points all the way through the bar exam three years later. And law school was expensive!

I opened the envelope and found a letter of congratulations instructing me to report to first-semester law school classes in August. Behind the letter was a stack of information for incoming students along with a hefty invoice. Staring at the contents of that envelope, what had been a whim just a few months ago suddenly got very real. It would have been much easier if FSU had just said no. That would have required no further action on my part. Now, I actually had to make a decision about whether I really wanted to go to law school after all. And if I did, how was I going to make that work? And how was I going to pay for it? I decided to tackle the second and third questions first.

FSU is located in Tallahassee, a two-hour drive from Panama City without traffic, and Tallahassee is in a different time zone to boot. Commuting daily, it turns out, was not a realistic option. Since I would have no source of income and since I would be returning to Panama City on weekends, I didn't relish the idea of spending money on a second housing arrangement, so I came up with an idea to have other students pay for my housing. I would buy the biggest house that I could afford that was near the law school in Tallahassee for the least amount of money per square foot, and I would rent out rooms to other students for enough money to cover my mortgage, insurance, taxes, maintenance, and living expenses. That idea plus the availability of financial aid to cover tuition solved both question two and question three in less than an hour.

When Tevye got home, I shared the news about my acceptance, and I also ran my house idea by him. Did he think that it could work? He was sure that it could. We spent the rest of the evening scheming over the particulars. I was very excited about the planning. It was like figuring out a puzzle, and I loved solving logistical puzzles. I got so wrapped up in the "how" that I never did get around to the question of "whether or not." Mentally, I just ran right over that question and barreled into full-on execution mode.

Within a week, I had found a four-bedroom, three-bathroom, two-story house with a large yard and a swimming pool. It had the square footage for a fifth bedroom and an easy floorplan in which to make that happen by erecting a single wall. Tevye agreed to help put up the wall, and he also volunteered to renovate one of the bathrooms while I worked on updating the kitchen to make the house attractive to other students.

Tevye and I worked together on the renovations during weekends throughout the summer, wearing out the highway between Panama City and Tallahassee and, even more so, the road between the house and the hardware store. For me, that summer was fondly reminiscent of the perpetual construction at Lake Pillsbury, and as hard as the work was, I loved it. When all of the renovations were complete, I found four other students to rent four of the bedrooms. I would stay in the fifth bedroom during the week, returning to Panama City on weekends. Having no good excuses left, I reported to first-semester law school classes in August of 2004.

Law school was miserable. From day one, first-year law students are instructed to take a long, hard look at themselves, because that might be the last time that they would ever see the person whom they were when they came in the door. Law school would profoundly change you, they said, and they made no secret about the fact that the change was not often for the better.

There were two choices of paths for law students. Most students assumed that the choice of paths was between litigation and transactional law, and that was indeed a choice that students would be required to make prior to graduation. But the true choice of paths that students had to make was whether they wanted to graduate in the top ten percent of their class or not. Students who graduated in the top ten percent got all of the best job offers from all of the big law firms and made all of the money right out of law school. If yours was the first name below the line separating out the top ten percent, most of the big law firms would not even grant you an interview.

For those students who wanted to be in the top ten percent, law school was toxically competitive. For every one student who made the top ten percent, nine very smart students did not, so you had to step on or over a lot of people if you were gunning for the top ten percent. For the smartest five percent of students, raw ability was sufficient. For the next ten percent, whether you rose to the top half of that group or not depended upon how ruthlessly you played the game. Pages would be ripped out of books in the library to prevent other students from reading required material. Notes from last year's exams were sold to the highest bidder. And professors would spend more time and effort coaching students whose parents had donated the most money to the law school or were otherwise considered elite. For those students who didn't care about being in the top ten percent, they could survive law school with their original selves intact. However, only about ten percent of students expected to be in the bottom ninety percent. That left a whole lot of anxiety in the middle.

It took me all of one semester to realize that I was not top ten percent material. First of all, I hadn't even been aware that being in the top ten percent was a thing, so I hadn't tried. Second of all, more than five percent of the other law students were smarter than me. And third of all, I had no interest in playing the game. I wrote well enough to get onto Law Review and to have two articles published, I argued well enough to get onto the Moot Court team, and I tested well enough to earn the number one score in several of my classes. But the stress was awful, and by the end of the first year, I just wanted to get the rest of law school over with and get out. I made a plan for that, stacking classes on top of two summer internships, and two-and-a-half years after my first August classes, I graduated from law school a full semester early.

CHAPTER TEN

The Bar Exam

From the day that I arrived on campus for my first law school class until the day that I graduated, the one consistent thing that had been drilled into me and my classmates by administrators, professors, and other law students was that it would be nearly impossible to pass the bar exam without taking the leading commercial bar exam prep course immediately following graduation. This course consisted of a series of in-person classes where law school graduates would sit, day after day, week after week, in a crowded, freezing-cold, hotel ballroom watching videos of someone reading exam review material to them. For this privilege, and for the lofty promise of the best and presumably only hope of passing the bar exam, students would eagerly fork over several thousand dollars to the for-profit monopoly that promoted the course.

This idea did not appeal to me in any way. For one thing, I hate being cold. Especially if that cold is blowing on me in the form of air conditioning. For another thing, I know how to read, and I can read on my own much faster than someone can read aloud to me on video. For a third thing, absent a compelling reason, I prefer for my money to be in my own pocket, rather than in somebody else's. Why on earth would I pay thousands of dollars to get up early in the morning, drive to a hotel, and be miserably cold all day, for days on end, all for the result of getting through the review material much more slowly than if

I were to simply read that same material myself in the comfort of my own home? It made no sense.

And so, much to the horror of my fellow classmates, who were certain that I was flushing my entire legal education and professional future down the drain, I took a hard pass on the commercial bar review course. Instead, I took a page out of the playbook that I had used to pass the securities licensing exams for the brokerage. I went online and purchased last year's used course materials off of ebay for less than a hundred bucks, and I read them myself. I also borrowed a set of cassette tapes of a supplementary audio course from one of my former housemates who had already passed the bar exam, and I listened to those tapes in my car while driving back and forth between Tallahassee and Panama City. This is how I studied for the bar exam.

None of this is meant to imply that studying for Florida's two-full-day bar exam was easy or that I took the task lightly. For those who haven't had the pleasure of sitting for a bar exam, these exams require near-encyclopedic memory of three years' worth of detailed cases, rules, and laws, the ability to recall which case, rule, or law applies to which type of situation, and the ability to recall and apply all of that information very, very quickly. Preparing for this type of exam involves extremely intense, extremely condensed study, and I was fully committed.

The trick to passing a bar exam (and other similarly rigorous licensing exams) is figuring out how to stuff the maximum amount of information into your brain in some sort of organized way and then hold it there long enough to get through the exam. If you start too late or don't put in enough reps each day, you won't be able to cram enough information into your brain in time. If you start too early or put in too many reps, you run the risk that the information that you input up front will leak out of the back before the exam date arrives. If you time everything just right, the information stays in your brain just long enough to get through the exam, and then it all spills out onto the pavement of the parking lot during the walk from the exam room door back to your car. By the time that you get to your car, you're lucky if you remember your own name.

Getting all of that information to stick in your brain requires strategically spaced periods of not studying, in much the same way that building physical muscle requires strategically spaced periods of rest. For me, this meant that each day, I had a few hours where it was imperative that I find something else for my brain to do. I had to purposely not think about cases or rules or laws or anything related to the bar exam during those hours, and ideally, I had to refrain from engaging in any additional kind of educational activity whatsoever, since available brain space was at a premium. I needed to be fully immersed in distraction of the entertainment variety.

The internet was a ready source of entertainment. There was all manner of rabbit holes available to go down that had nothing at all to do with education or with studying for the bar exam. I watched movies, scrolled through travel sites, and geeked out on home remodeling before-and-after photos. I also stumbled into the brave new world of online matchmaking websites. These sites were just starting to gain traction in mainstream America in the early 2000s, before social media was a thing, and I found them fascinating. Not only could you scroll through photos, but you could actually strike up conversations with complete strangers. The more reputable sites had "just friends" categories, which seemed like a pretty low risk way to go, so I set up a couple of accounts and met all kinds of new "friends" who would recount endless details about their individual interests, none of which involved studying for the bar exam.

One of the friends that I met who particularly intrigued me was named Amanda. Amanda lived a few hours away from me in Florida, and she had just broken up with her girlfriend. Amanda had been in an unhappy marriage with the father of her teenage daughter when she had met this girlfriend. She hadn't been looking for a relationship with anyone, much less with a woman, but Amanda had found this woman irresistible, and she had left her husband to be with her. The relationship didn't last, but the experience had opened up a whole new world for Amanda. Now that she was on her own, Amanda was eager to explore her new-found freedom and to have more experiences with women. Amanda wanted to know what I thought about that.

I didn't know what I thought about that. Other than what I had felt for Naomi, I hadn't given that kind of thing much thought. But now that I had been asked what I thought about it, I clicked back through the files of my mind, and I discovered all sorts of times when I had felt attraction toward women. I had assumed that I was just attracted to their personality, in a friend sort of way. But what if that wasn't it at all? What if that attraction was sexual? What if I were actually gay? Could that be why nothing seemed to be working out for me with men? Maybe I should find out. Maybe it was necessary for me to find out. I made arrangements to meet up with Amanda in a town midway between where each of us lived.

The meeting with Amanda was disappointing. Amanda spent much of the time on her phone texting with her ex-girlfriend whom, it turned out, wasn't quite as "ex" as she had led me to believe. In between those texts, Amanda let me know that she was open to a one-and-done type of interaction with me, but that she planned to drive home the next morning to spend Valentine's Day with her not-so-ex-girlfriend. That proposition struck me as all kinds of heartache waiting to happen. So, I wished Amanda well, made my way back to Tallahassee, and turned my attention to less hazardous forms of entertainment while I continued to study for the bar exam. However, the lid of Pandora's box had been lifted for me, even if just a crack, and thoughts of what might have happened with Amanda persisted in my mind.

During my exam prep time, I also had to make a decision about where I wanted to work as a lawyer. I had interviewed with a leading firm in Panama City where Tevye lived, but I concluded that a small town that was best known as a spring break destination held little for me in the way of a legal future. Tevye had been incredibly supportive all through law school, but it was time for me to leave his nest and see if my newly-developed wings would hold my weight. I had two other offers on the table that I was seriously considering. One was in Tampa, and one was in Fort Lauderdale. Each had its own merits, and I was hard pressed to decide between the two. The decision ultimately came down to the fact that I knew a total of one person in Fort Lauderdale and a total of zero people in Tampa. Fort Lauderdale was the winner.

Nearly all job offers made to third-year law students are contingent upon the student obtaining a passing score on the bar exam, usually on the first attempt. This is not a given. In February of 2007, when I took the Florida bar exam, the pass rate was 56%. February pass rates were typically lower than pass rates in July, the one other time of year when the bar exam is offered. July pass rates in Florida tended to hover around 70%. Lower pass rates in February were partially due to a skewed percentage of test-takers who had not passed the more populous July exam the previous year, and partially due to a heavier concentration of test-takers who had not matriculated through law school at the usual time or in the usual way — those graduates who were older career-changers or who had taken either more or less time than the prescribed three years to complete law school. Graduates like me.

The day of the bar exam arrived, and I was ready. I had taken dozens of practice tests and had been consistently scoring above where I needed to be. When the doors opened, I walked into the enormous hotel ballroom full of rows and rows of tables, located my seat, and waited with nervous confidence for the proctor to start the test. When the second hand on the room's big clock ticked around to nine a.m., the proctor announced, "You may begin." I opened my test booklet, took a deep, calming breath, and dove in.

About an hour into the exam, one of the examinees a few tables in front of me passed out. He just tipped right over onto the floor, unconscious. Hotel staff ran over there. Security ran over there. All of the staff were whispering frantically. The exam did not stop. "Please keep your eyes on your own exams," was the only announcement that the proctor made. A few minutes later, paramedics rushed in and wheeled the examinee away on a stretcher.

About another hour into the exam, a girl at the table next to mine began to weep. She didn't get up, she didn't put her head down, she just kept on testing and weeping and occasionally blowing her nose. "Please keep your eyes on your own exams," the proctor repeated.

Upon returning from each break, more and more chairs would be empty that had previously been occupied. Occupied by examinees who just didn't come back from the break.

From the moment that I walked out of the exam room at the end of the second day, I was certain that I hadn't passed. I knew for sure that I had totally bombed one of the essays, and there were only four of those. Plus, I had been completely clueless about a whole swath of the multiple choice questions. But the biggest indication that I hadn't passed was that in a giant ballroom full of hundreds of examinees, I was one of the first few students to turn in my answer packet and walk out of the room during each of the four sessions. I had nothing left to add to any of my answers, while all of my classmates who had paid thousands of dollars for the commercial bar review course kept right on writing and typing until they were ordered to stop. Clearly, I was missing something significant. It seemed that everyone had been right about the bar review course after all, and I had blown it.

In Florida, as in nearly all states, there was a several-month delay between the time that the bar exam was administered and the time that results were published. The purpose of this delay was to give the examiners time to review the written, essay-type responses by hand. On the day that bar exam results were scheduled to be published, I was working in Fort Lauderdale in the office of the Public Defender, protecting the rights of juvenile offenders under a provisional law license granted to public servants whose permanent licenses were pending bar exam results. The air was tense that day as my fellow provisional licensees spent the morning continuously refreshing the portal on the website where exam results were set be published. Just before lunch time, the office erupted in chaos. Bar exam results had been posted to the portal, and everyone was frantically searching for their identification number and for their results, knowing that these results would determine their near-term fate. Those who learned that they had passed collided in a huddle, high-fived each other, and headed out to lunch to celebrate. Those who had not passed either slumped at their desk and sobbed or slipped quietly out the back door.

I kept working. I didn't want to look at the website. Like Schrödinger and his cat, so long as I didn't check the website, my results could either be "pass" or not. As soon as I checked, I would be stuck with the results, one way or the other.

Later that afternoon, my boss walked by and stuck his head in my door.

"So?" he asked.

"I don't know yet," I responded.

"What do you mean you don't know?"

"I haven't checked yet."

"Well, check!" he said.

"I will," I replied, "just as soon as I finish prepping for tomorrow morning's hearings."

"Check!" he commanded.

"Okay!" I promised, holding his gaze until he walked away.

I continued working on my hearing prep.

After the bar exam, I had gotten together with a few of my peers from law school for an evening of celebration and wishing one another well. Several of the conversations that evening had revolved around the exam's essay questions. The last thing that I had wanted to do that evening was to talk about bar exam material! But there was no escaping the topic. The more that I listened to how my classmates had answered those questions, the more certain I had become that I had definitely not passed.

Toward the end of the work day, my boss came back again.

"So?" he inquired.

"I'll check tonight," I replied.

He stared at me, dumbfounded. Eventually, he walked away, shaking his head.

After I had finished preparing for the next day's hearings, I organized all of my files, and then I tidied up my office. When I had inherited that office and those same files from my predecessor, they were a mess. I didn't want to leave a similar mess for the next person. It wasn't fair to that person, and it wouldn't be fair to all of the young people that each of those files represented who had no one else to defend their rights.

Finally, after there was nothing left to tidy up and I had packed my bag to go home, I sat down at the computer, took a deep breath, and logged on to the portal. I scrolled and scrolled and finally found my number. There were three columns to the right of the column with the numbers. One column displayed the multiple choice results, one column displayed the essay results, and one column provided the overall exam results. You had to pass both the multiple choice section and the essay section in order to pass the overall exam. Failing either would result in failure overall.

My eyes traced a horizontal line from left to right, starting with my number. Pass, pass, pass. I was stunned. Wait a minute, that must not be my number. I rechecked the number. Checked every digit, backwards and forwards. I had read it right, that was my number. Maybe I hadn't tracked across the line properly. Maybe I had jumped a row. Without taking my eyes off of the screen, I reached into my file drawer and grabbed a random piece of paper from a folder. I pressed the paper up against the screen, lined it up horizontally with my number, and made sure that I was holding it exactly straight and level. Pass, pass, pass.

Oh my gosh! No way! NO WAY!!! I passed the $%)*&# bar exam!
And then...
Oh, wow... Now I have to be a lawyer...

CHAPTER ELEVEN

Liberty and Justice for All

Serving as a public defender, first with juveniles and then with adults, was the greatest honor of my legal career. It was also the one job for which I have received the most judgment and the greatest condemnation from others – some well-meaning, some not. The criticisms ranged anywhere from asking why someone who did so well in a top tier law school would "settle" for one of the least respected, lowest paying jobs in the industry, to asking how I could stand to live with myself while defending these awful, evil criminals. The questions dripped with undisguised disgust. Criminal defense was the only category of lawyer deemed morally lower than "ambulance-chaser." At least "ambulance-chasers" were paid well.

Those who gave me the benefit of the doubt invented their own rationale for my choice. I must have been doing it because, every once in a while, someone is innocent. I must have been trying to find and help the innocent people, they assumed. But the question inevitably would follow of how I could possibly defend someone whom I knew in my heart was guilty, and then the same disgust would surface.

I had two reasons for choosing to serve as a public defender. The first reason, which I would share with those few who genuinely cared to know, was that I fiercely believed in the rights that led our country's founding fathers to reject the tyranny of monarchy and to build a country based on the constitutional principles of liberty and justice for all. These rights mean that government representatives don't just get to accuse you or me at random of committing some crime and then search us, take away our belongings, and imprison us at will. There actually has to be evidence of some probability that a crime has been committed by us before they can search us and take our things, and then a group of our peers must determine within a reasonable amount of time and beyond a reasonable doubt, based upon relevant evidence, that it was indeed you or I who committed said crime before we can be incarcerated. If those rights aren't afforded to everyone, then neither you nor I can count on them being afforded to us if we were to find ourselves accused of a crime. I didn't defend crimes. I defended rights. And I was very good at it.

The second reason, which I seldom shared because no one wanted to hear it, was that even though I had estranged myself from God, I still believed in mercy and grace. This does not mean that I didn't believe in consequences. When someone commits a crime, there are consequences that result from that crime. While genuine repentance and seeking forgiveness are the beginning of healing, they don't erase the consequences. There are consequences for the person who committed the crime, and there are consequences for the people who were hurt by that crime, and everyone has to live with those consequences, often for the rest of their lives.

That said, people screw up. Sometimes really badly. I certainly have. There's not a single one of us who hasn't. Some screw-ups are intentional, and some screw-ups are just plain dumb. Some people get caught, and some people get lucky. I dealt with the ones who got caught.

No one can do anything to change what happened yesterday, but every one of us can decide who we want to be today and tomorrow. Even criminals. Even the worst ones. The people that I dealt with needed somebody to believe that with them. To help them to find purpose in a life that is bounded by, but not bound by, the consequences of their actions. To help them to stand up and show up tomorrow, and the day after that. I could do that with them. I would do that with them. And for some of them, I was the only one in their life who would.

For me, the problem with serving as a public defender wasn't all of those reasons that everyone spat at me. The problem was that there was not enough time to care. Just doing the bare minimum meant late nights at the office and/or taking work home plus spending at least one day of nearly every weekend in jail. I have probably spent more time sitting in jail than some of the defendants that I represented.

I will always remember one Saturday morning in the juvenile detention center where I met a young client named Jesse for the first time. Jesse was sixteen years old, and he was being held on charges of assault and multiple counts of child endangerment. Jesse had been arrested after he had opened the emergency door in the back of a moving school bus, jumped out, and run away following a verbal altercation with another kid on the bus. I asked Jesse to talk with me about what had happened.

Most of the time, when I would ask clients to describe what happened, I would hear some version of a story so wildly unbelievable that it was all I could do not to burst out laughing. One memorable example was the client who admitted that the drug paraphernalia that police had found in his pocket belonged to him but said that he had no idea how the bag of crack that was found inserted into his backside had gotten there. He swore that he was as surprised as anybody, and he was adamant that it definitely was not his!

Jesse's story was not like those stories. When I asked Jesse what happened on the bus, he replied simply, "I was having an emergency, so I went out the emergency exit."

I pressed him to elaborate.

"Sometimes I get real mad," Jesse said, "and when I get mad, I hit people. Like when my dad hits my mom, only harder."

Jesse went on. "I'm not a little kid anymore. I'm sixteen now. And I'm big. Big like my dad."

Jesse paused, then he added, "My dad hit somebody, and they died, and now my dad is in prison."

Jesse continued. "I was getting real mad at this kid. I kept getting madder and madder, and I just knew that if I didn't get out of that bus right now, I was gonna hit him. I wanted to kill that kid. And I could have. I asked the bus driver to stop. I begged him. But he wouldn't stop. Don't you understand? I just had to get out of there, but the driver wouldn't stop. So, I went out the back."

Jesse ended, sobbing, "I don't wanna be like my dad."

Jesse was ultimately convicted as charged, but I worked hard to get both him and his mother connected with services that could help them. For years after that, I continued to receive letters and drawings that Jesse would send to me from detention.

For those public defenders who took the time to care, to listen to their clients, to seek out resources that their clients needed in order to heal, or to communicate with their clients' families, all hope of having any kind of personal life went completely out the window. What little personal time there was would be spent using any means possible to forget about the problems of the two-hundred-plus clients that each of us was charged with defending. This led to a lot of very intense partying and a lot of very intense drinking, and I was no exception.

My apartment was located within walking distance of Wilton Drive, the main drag in the town of Wilton Manors, which itself is wrapped around by the north end of the city of Fort Lauderdale. The town of roughly eleven thousand people prides itself as being the "second-gayest city" in America, trailing only Provincetown, Massachusetts, in the number of individuals per capita who identify as LGBTQ. Wilton Drive is lined on both sides with restaurants, bars, and clubs catering to the gay community, and from happy hour until closing time, the sidewalks would be packed with young and not-so-young revelers who were out people-watching while hopping from bar to bar and from club to club.

After my experience with Amanda had cracked open the Pandora's box of non-traditional sexuality, I knew that I needed to look inside. I had spent all of my life running away from difficult or confusing emotions. If I was ever going to learn who I was, I needed to tackle those emotions, and this was a big one. I didn't know where or how to begin, but I figured that Wilton Drive was as good a place as any to observe the gay community in action. Maybe I would even give a few experiences a try.

Most bars and clubs on Wilton Drive either had mixed clientele or catered primarily to men, but one popular bar catered mostly to women, and I spent quite a bit of time there. At first, I was terrified to talk with anyone. It seemed like everyone there knew everyone else, and everyone there looked the same, dressed the same way, and wore their hair the same way. Everyone except for me. As I sat at the bar, I felt like a giant spotlight was shining down on me. "Imposter! Not one of us! Doesn't belong here!" is what I was sure the spotlight was screaming. Every instinct told me to get out of there. To run. But I had to stay. I had to know.

To keep myself glued to my seat, I ordered round after round of drinks. Top-shelf tequila was my poison, straight up. In between shots, I would drink a beer to slow down the process of intoxication. As the drinks kept coming, I found it easier and easier to talk with people, and I became less and less concerned about what they might think.

As it turns out, there was a spotlight shining on me, but it was not the one that I had thought. "New girl!" the spotlight shouted, and it brought me all kinds of attention. Most of the attention came from really nice women who genuinely wanted to welcome me to the neighborhood. Some of the attention came from women who were more interested in being a private welcoming committee of one. Subconsciously, this felt like good attention, just as it had at the brokerage. It also facilitated my desire to have experiences with women. I had a new experience almost every night. None of them lasted for more than one night, and I was fine with that. I wasn't looking for a deep, emotional connection with anyone else at that point. I was still trying to connect with myself.

Beyond my nightly shenanigans, I made several friends at the bar as well, and I soon found myself hanging out with my new friends outside of Wilton Drive, playing softball in the gay league on Sunday mornings and spending weekend afternoons poolside at friends' homes, enjoying the sunshine and good company. The group that I grew closest to was a mix of young and old of all colors, backgrounds and professions. Most were women, but male friends were welcome, and children were nearly always present on Sundays. We called ourselves the Circle of Friends, or COF for short, and many of us got matching rainbow-colored COF tattoos.

The COF was a warm and welcoming group, and they made me feel at home in a town where I knew no one. (The one person I had known from law school had moved away shortly after I arrived.) I was new to the world of gayness, and my new friends helped me to navigate the ropes. I learned to wear my clothing and style my hair to fit in, use people's preferred pronouns, figure out who was attached to whom, and steer away from the drama that seemed to bubble up in direct correlation with the flowing of alcohol. Between living in Wilton Manors and hanging out with the COF, there was little need to venture outside of the "gayborhood" for anything other than work.

It wasn't long before I had a girlfriend. Or at least, kind of a girlfriend. She never did decide if she wanted to use that word. I'm not sure whether she was all that fond of me, but she was fond of being coupled, so we spent quite a bit of time together. By the time that I met her, I had already had experiences with many women, but this was the first one that had lasted for more than one night. After a few short months of dating, our relationship reverted to the "just friends" category, a casualty of drama involving yet another not-so-ex-girlfriend. But in all of those experiences, I had arrived at the conclusion that yes, I definitely was gay.

I had mixed emotions about this. On the one hand, I felt relief and a sense of accomplishment about having handled one huge rock. I had tackled and resolved a big question about my identity. Being gay seemed to make sense of why my relationships with men had failed. It also gave me a place to belong again. The gay community was full of people who had been grappling with issues of identity their whole lives. They understood my struggles, and they welcomed me with compassion and grace on a deeper level than I had previously experienced with anyone other than Tevye.

On the other hand, I didn't know how to reconcile being gay with the faith that remained within me. I still wasn't speaking to God, but somehow, the Word continued to reside deep inside me, and living a gay lifestyle and feelings of gayness brought with them a constant spiritual dissonance churning beneath the surface. I wasn't ready to deal with that dissonance yet, so I disconnected from those feelings and remained safely on the surface of gayness.

Around that same time, I left the public defender's office. The combination of an impossible caseload and shamefully low pay led to a statistically high burnout rate among public defenders. It took me less than a year to become a statistic. I just couldn't abide an environment where, in order to survive, much less ever hope to be successful, I had to stop caring, or at least stop caring as much.

When I started looking for different legal work, I came across an advertisement for a "real estate law" position. The position required some litigation experience, but not much. The job was closer to my apartment, it paid much better, and it didn't require spending any time in jail. That last part alone would be a welcome upgrade! I applied, interviewed, and got the job.

This was in the fall of 2007, and the nationwide mortgage meltdown was just beginning to heat up. Loan originators had created a money machine by packaging up as many loans as possible and selling them as securities to investors. When the pool of qualified borrowers had started to dry up, loan originators had duped sub-prime borrowers into taking out loans that they didn't understand, turning a blind eye toward those borrowers' lack of ability to repay that type of loan. By the time that those loans went south, the loan originators had made their money, and the investors were left holding the bag.

As the mortgage crisis worsened and began to take the economy and the job market down with it, many desperate borrowers legitimately could not afford to pay their home loans anymore and sought relief in the courts. Other less scrupulous borrowers and their attorneys simply gamed the system, knowing that court dockets were so backed up that they could take advantage of this situation to live in their home for free for years and then just walk away. It was up to the investors and the lawyers and the courts to sort it all out.

I found out in a hurry that the advertised "real estate law" job meant taking houses away from borrowers who hadn't kept up with their mortgage payments. I traveled to courts in counties all over the state to conduct hearings foreclosing on people's homes. It was not unusual for me to handle over one hundred hearings in a single day. The typical hearing would last less than five minutes. The borrowers never won. The best that they or their attorneys could hope to do was to kick the can a little bit further down the road.

Legally, the outcomes were correct: If you borrow money from someone to buy something and you promise to pay the money back, and you also promise the person that if you don't pay the money back, they can have the thing that you bought, then you either have to pay the money back or the person gets to keep the thing that you bought. You don't get to keep both somebody else's money and the thing that you bought with it. The rules aren't different if the thing that you bought is a house. Still, watching family after family walk into the courtroom with no money, no job, and no plan B, and walk out of the courtroom with no hope and no home, was heartbreaking.

Eventually, I had had enough. Being a lawyer was never supposed to be heartbreaking, yet that's all that it had been since day one. There were thousands of families every day who were losing their homes with no place to go, and there was nothing that I could do to help them. There were thousands of kids like Jesse who were unlikely to break out of the cycle of crime and imprisonment, no matter what I did. I determined to find some kind of law that I could practice that wasn't heartbreaking.

I thought back through all of the classes that I had taken in law school. Estate planning seemed like a good candidate. Estate planning wouldn't be heartbreaking. Boring maybe, but not heartbreaking. I wouldn't have to sign up to handle the back end when people died, I could just draft the documents on the front end. So, I enrolled in an intensive, bootcamp-type, refresher course on estate planning, gave notice at the "real estate law" firm, and hung out a shingle of my own. Now I was not only an estate planning attorney, I was also a small business owner.

CHAPTER TWELVE

Father's Day

The law firm that I opened was specifically designed to fill a niche in the community where I lived: estate planning for unmarried couples. In 2008, gay marriage was not legal in Florida, nor was it legal in the United States in general. This meant that gay couples wanting to plan together had to be intentional about how they set up things like powers of attorney and related testamentary documents, since it was not uncommon for family members to contest a person's wishes to leave an inheritance to their partner or to allow their partner to visit them in the hospital or to make medical or financial decisions on their behalf. In addition to serving the gay community, my firm also served the unmarried senior community at large, primarily widows and widowers who had found love again but who didn't want to take the hit to social security and other government benefits that was often a financial penalty of remarrying.

I have always had an entrepreneurial inclination, and starting a law firm fed that appetite in me. I built a strong brand and established a network of connections and became an active member of my community. Through this process, I met clients and business associates and new friends and sometimes dating partners.

There is a joke that is well-known among the gay community: "What does a lesbian bring with her on a second date? A U-Haul." This joke made me uncomfortable, but I also found it to be based on at least a kernel of truth. I developed a couple of longer-term, live-in relationships, but they were emotionally shallow, and each ended up coming unglued over some form of drama or another. Both times, I was relieved to be rid of the drama.

The thing that made me uncomfortable about the U-Haul joke was not that it stereotyped a behavior. It was its use of the term "lesbian." I never liked the word, and I never used it to describe myself. I didn't understand why the word "gay" was used as an adjective when describing men, but for women, the word "lesbian" was nearly always used as a noun. For men, people say, "A gay man." "He is gay." For women, they say "She is a lesbian," not, "She is lesbian." "A lesbian woman" would be considered redundant.

This bothered me for reasons that went beyond an anomaly of grammar. Adjectives describe. Nouns define. Adjectives illustrate one of many aspects of a person. Nouns label the whole person. Nouns bestow identity. I was still getting used to "gay" as an adjective to describe me. I did not want any term that revolved around sexuality to define me. My identity was still eluding me, but the defining essence of who I was as a person would not be grounded in that.

––––––––

To say that my parents were not thrilled with my new lifestyle would be an understatement. They were dismayed. Their daughter had abandoned Christianity, divorced a perfectly good husband, left a nice, safe career with health insurance and a 401(k), moved to the other end of the country, lived for a time with a man twenty-five years her senior doing God-knows-what, and now she had come out as gay. My parents were not only disappointed in me, they feared for my soul. Had I ever really been a Christian? Was I now? They didn't know, and those questions haunted them.

One spring Sunday evening, I received a phone call from my parents. I would often receive calls from Mom, and sometimes from Dad, but it was very rare that both of them would call me together, and when they did, it was never good. Dad's cancer had come back. He had been fighting prostate cancer on and off for years with a good measure of success, but the form of prostate cancer that ran in his family was particularly aggressive, and it had now taken hold and was spreading to other parts of his body. He was comfortable and happy and living life vibrantly, but his remaining time was limited.

I hung up the phone after that conversation, dumfounded and in shock. Dad's original cancer diagnosis had come decades ago. He had had the surgery, radiation, and chemo. He had followed all of the doctors' instructions. He and Mom and their whole church had prayed. And Dad's cancer had become undetectable. Sure, over the years, his PSA numbers had elevated slightly above zero, but it was nothing to be concerned about, the doctors had assured us.

My father had always been vibrant and strong. Invincible. He was the Air Force war veteran. The provider. The builder of cabins. The killer of snakes and spiders. The rescuer of me. And now, he was dying. How was this possible? I hadn't realized until that phone call that I had never imagined a life without my parents. Without my father at the helm of the family. It felt like someone had just lit my safety net on fire.

I thought about my current life in Florida. What did I have there, really? I had a law firm that was finally starting to get solid traction, but it wasn't yet to the point where it was thriving. I had friends whom I enjoyed spending time with, but I didn't have any truly close relationships. The people who were most important to me in my life had been on the other end of that phone call, and one of them didn't have very much time left. The decision was made. Over the next few weeks, I referred my clients out, closed up my business, loaded my belongings and my pets into a rented yellow truck, drove my SUV up onto the attached car trailer, and headed west.

Prior to leaving Florida, I had reached out to a dear family friend named Larry who lived in the small mountain town of Twain Harte, California, where my parents had retired. I let Larry know that I would be moving to Twain Harte, and that I wanted to surprise my parents. I had rented a little cabin that I had found online, and I asked Larry if he could help me to organize some help with unloading the moving truck when I arrived and then accompany me to my parents' house to surprise them. Larry was elated to be in on the surprise, and he was eager to help.

I arrived in Twain Harte on Father's Day in 2012. After Larry and I and some teenagers from Larry's church got the moving truck unloaded, Larry followed me in his pickup to drop off the moving truck and car trailer at the rental location on the receiving end, and then he drove me over to my parents' house, where he had already been invited to join them for dinner.

Rounding the bend of my parents' long driveway, we spotted my dad at the top of the hill, carrying a giant basket of vegetables into his workshop in the third bay of my parents' garage. As Larry pulled his pickup into the parking area at the top of the driveway, Dad set down his basket and walked out to greet Larry. When Dad saw me tumble out of the passenger's side of Larry's pickup, he stopped. He just stood there, staring at me in disbelief.

"Happy Father's Day!" I proclaimed as I bounded over and gave Dad a huge hug. Dad wrapped his arms so tightly around me that he squeezed the breath out of me. We both cried. Inside, my mom was equally surprised, and after more hugs and more tears, she shifted into full-on mom-mode and bustled about the kitchen, happily setting another place at the table.

Mom was an amazing cook, and she always made enough food to feed an army. If you didn't have heaping mounds of seconds, she was hurt. But the crown jewel of summer dinners at my parents' house was always the salad. Dad was a master gardener and had installed a huge, fenced, three-tiered garden on their hillside property, along with a hothouse for starting seedlings in the spring. The garden was equal parts landscape architecture and engineering genius. Each tier measured eight feet by twenty-four feet, and two of the three tiers were filled with every kind of vegetable, with multiple varieties of many of them. The third tier was entirely dedicated to growing roses and other flowers for my mom. Each evening, Dad would pick vegetables about a half an hour before dinner, and he would bring them through his shop and into the house, where he would make the most incredibly complex fresh salads that I have ever eaten.

After we all enjoyed a hearty dinner of barbequed chicken, corn bread, home-made baked beans, lightly-steamed spinach, and of course a second helping of Dad's wonderful salad, Mom brought out a warm, fresh-baked apple pie and served it along with her favorite: vanilla ice cream. The dinner conversation thus far had been all about what was happening in their world and what had been happening in mine, but I kept steering away from tales of my trip west, waiting for the right moment to reveal the big surprise. Up to that point, all that my parents knew was that I had come for a Father's Day visit.

Once Mom made sure that everyone had received a large slice of pie and an over-sized helping of ice cream, she lifted her fork – the universal signal, handed down through generations of etiquette in her family – indicating that we all should eat. As we savored our first sweet bites, Mom raised the topic of making up the bed in the guest bedroom for me to sleep in, and that's when I told her that there was no need, I had a place to stay.

She and Dad set their forks down and looked at each other, con-fused and a little concerned. They both were very active in their church, and so was Larry, and I think that they were trying to wrap their heads around why I would be staying at Larry's house.

"It's okay, Mom, I live here now."

More confusion on their faces. More concern. Could it be that I was planning to move in with Larry, a single, Christian man who was fifteen years older than me?

"Mom, I rented a little cabin, right up the road. Just a mile away. I moved in today. I live here now."

More silence.

"Happy Father's Day!" I added, flashing a Cheshire-cat grin.

The tears and cries of astonishment eclipsed the apple pie. My parents were thrilled. I was thrilled. All of the ice cream melted. It didn't matter. Their prodigal daughter had come back home. They didn't quite know what to make of all that was happening, but in the moment, it didn't matter. We drank in the rest of that lovely summer evening with the assurance that there would be many more. When it was finally time for Larry to take me back to my little cabin, I hopped into the passenger's seat of his pickup and looked up to see my parents standing in the driveway, arm-in-arm, waving goodbye. They have always done that – waved goodbye from the driveway – ever since the day that I left home at age eighteen to drive south to USC. But this time, it was a happy goodbye. I would see them again for dinner the next evening, and so many evenings after that.

Those evenings with my parents were incredibly special. I would work from my little rented cabin all day doing contract legal work for a client in Florida, and then after work I would head over to my parents' house to join them for dinner and to watch the San Francisco Giants play baseball on TV. The Giants were having a great season, and we did our part to cheer them on. Matt Cain had pitched a perfect game while I was driving from Florida to California, and the team was in the middle of a five-year dynasty that would include three World Series as well as two no-hitters for Timmy Lincecum. Rooting for "our boys" was something that we could all agree on. On travel days for the team, my parents would tune the TV to *Jeopardy!* and *Wheel of Fortune*, and we would all chime in along with the contestants to guess the answers. The conversations never went deep during those evenings, we just enjoyed the presence of one another's company.

As devout evangelical Christians, my parents had struggled with many of the choices that I had made in my life, most especially my lifestyle. But they loved me unconditionally, and they had always made sure that I knew that and felt that from them. Above all, they didn't want to do or say anything that would risk pushing me away. Especially now that they had me back within arms' reach. They let me know that I was welcome to attend church with them, but they didn't push, and they introduced me to all of their friends

One Saturday afternoon, my parents took me with them to visit a couple of their closest friends. The husband invited my dad to step outdoors with him to have a look at a piece of farm equipment that the husband had just bought. I was interested and wanted to go with them. However, I was not invited. I was to stay indoors with the women. The wife was eager to show me her quilting room. I had no interest whatsoever in quilting, but I followed along dutifully to see the quilting room, and then I sat in the formal living room with the wife and my mom for what seemed like an eternity, drinking iced tea and talking about quilting clubs and looking through endless photo albums of other people's grandchildren.

When the men finally came back, I could not get out of there fast enough. Being back in the safety of my parents' nest came with a price: I felt like I was being pushed back down into the prescribed role for what little girls are to become. Men work with farm equipment. Women sew quilts and drink iced tea and talk about children. Men do the real work. Women stay in the background and support their men. These roles are non-negotiable. And women certainly don't partner up with other women. I felt like a fish out of water in this tiny mountain town of mostly white, conservative, evangelical Christians. Having just come from south Florida where white people, conservatives, and evangelical Christians were in the minority, I was experiencing serious culture shock.

After that day, I was determined to find "my people." Not surprisingly, the gay community was pretty much non-existent in my new town, but about an hour's drive west, in California's central valley, there was a bit more of a population. I got online and did a little research, and before long, I had found at least couple of places where I could go to get a dose of "my people" from time to time.

For the most part, though, I was happy living in my little mountain community, and I would not have traded that time with my parents for anything.

CHAPTER THIRTEEN

Little Adult

My parents met each other in college after Dad had returned from four years of combat service in the Air Force during the Korean War. Dad had been just a young boy, the middle of three brothers, when his White father and half-Cherokee mother divorced. Dad's father soon remarried, and Dad was struggling to adjust to those changes, so he spent much of his childhood living with his paternal grandparents in rural, agricultural, central California while his two brothers lived with my grandfather, Grandpa's second wife, and their new baby in suburban San Mateo. After graduating from high school, with the draft looming, Dad enlisted in the Air Force on the theory that it had a slightly higher survival rate than the Army that he would likely have been drafted into.

Mom was the eldest of five siblings and was raised in suburban Michigan near Detroit. Her parents had a complicated marriage that was strained by an imbalance of familial wealth and the despair of having lost their own wealth during the Great Depression. Due to a health condition, Mom spent most of her childhood summers at the lakeside summer home of her wealthy maternal grandparents, a privilege that her siblings did not enjoy. Mom's grandparents employed several Black servants who loved my mother and whom she loved in return. However, the impression that this environment imprinted upon my mother's young life would forever color her view of the hierarchy of race in America.

Mom and Dad began their married lives together in 1958 in the heart of the rapidly growing technology hub that would soon become known as Silicon Valley. Dad had graduated with a degree in architectural engineering, and there was no shortage of work for a young man with the skills to design high-tech research facilities and clean manufacturing plants. He accepted an offer to work for Lockheed, which had recently moved its headquarters from southern California to Sunnyvale.

Job prospects for female college graduates were another story. Mom had graduated near the top of her class with a degree in philosophy and a minor in interior design. However, for women in the 1950s, college was best known as an avenue to obtain an "MRS" degree, and that had been Mom's goal. Now happily married, Mom found work that she enjoyed as a principal's secretary in the local school system, and she also volunteered with the church that she and Dad attended.

The newlyweds spent their evenings and weekends in the company of good friends, often playing cards in bridge tournaments, usually drinking martinis and Manhattans, and always smoking. Before they married, Mom and Dad had made the deliberate decision to spend the first several years of their marriage simply as a married couple. They wanted to take the time to enjoy that season of their lives, and equally importantly, they wanted to be intentional about building a strong foundation in their marriage before introducing children into the mix.

When my parents decided that the time was right to start a family, they did everything that they could to be well prepared. They had been carefully incubating a small financial nest egg and had saved nearly enough money for a down payment on a house. They researched the best neighborhood schools within a reasonable commute from Dad's workplace. They both stopped smoking. They practically memorized Dr. Spock's popular book, *Baby and Child Care*, which at the time had sold the second-most copies of any book in American history, behind only the Bible.

When Mom got pregnant with me, my parents attended Lamaze childbirth classes together. They purchased the cradle and the crib and the playpen and the changing table and the high chair and the stroller and all of the things that a family with a new baby would need. They hired a service that would come once a week to deliver clean cloth diapers and take away the soiled ones. They hired Nora, a widowed cafeteria lady from Mom's school, to be ready to help Mom with cooking and mothering and housekeeping chores during the afternoons.

Once I was born and my parents finally brought me home after those harrowing couple of weeks in the NICU, life was good for Cliff and Marty Simpson. Dad's father had counseled him to buy the most house that they could possibly afford on Dad's salary, reasoning that with time, Dad's salary would increase, but their house payment would stay the same. Dad took that advice, and our budding family soon moved into the four-bedroom, two-bathroom home where I grew up. Mom started smoking again when I graduated from breast-feeding to solid food, but she stopped again when she became pregnant with my sister, and she stayed stopped after that.

My parents had agreed that Mom would quit her job shortly before I was born so that she could spend all of her time raising their children. As our little family grew from three to four with the birth of my younger sister, Dad was doing the best that he could on his modest salary to make the mortgage payments and pay the rest of the bills and keep up with expenses and buy all of the things that infants and toddlers and new mothers require. When Dad had taken his father's advice and bought the house, he had known that the mortgage payments would be a stretch, but with a family that was growing faster than his salary, it was becoming evident that additional income would be needed.

Mom and Dad both had been adamant that their children would be raised by their mother and not by a stranger. They both also had been adamant that their children would have a father who was present and an active part of their children's daily lives. And so, rather than Dad taking on a second job or Mom taking a job outside of the home, Mom took additional children into our home and cared for those children while their parents worked. Thus was born our "Daytime Family."

The Daytime Family fluctuated from around five to eight kids at a time, all between my sister's and my ages. Mark, Tom and Carole were everyday kids, and Sherry, Kristie, Craig, Donny, and Steven would cycle through fairly regularly on an as-needed basis. In addition to the Daytime Family, our house always seemed to be full of neighborhood kids. Kim, Mike, Kimo, Stephanie, and my best friend Jennie were regulars. I could not have asked for a better environment to grow up in than having all of those kids around, having my own mother there, and having my father come home for dinner every night. We lived in Mayberry, and we were the Cleavers.

Like all parents, Mom and Dad made the most of what they had and what they knew to raise my sister and me. And, like all parents, they weren't perfect. One of the downsides to having all of those kids around all the time was that my sister and I had very little one-on-one time with our parents. By the time that Dad got home from work, Mom was hungry for adult conversation, and Dad was just plain hungry. Between dinner, martinis and Manhattans, the CBS Evening News with Walter Cronkite, and adult conversation, there never seemed to be much opportunity for any depth of interaction between my parents and me. There was the usual "How was school?" type of dialogue, but not much along the lines of "How did that make you feel?" or "What do you think about that?" Dr. Spock's book had taught my parents to let their kids think independently, and my sister and I had plenty of opportunity to do just that.

You would think that with all of those kids around all the time, I would have developed strong social skills at a young age. The opposite was true. Most of the time, I was the oldest kid in the Daytime Family, and much of the time, Mom simply didn't have enough hands to corral that many children effectively. This meant that I was often asked to step up and be the other adult in the room with kids who were only a year or two younger than me. I craved Mom's attention, so I did everything that I could to make her proud. The happiest words that I would hear were when Mom bragged to her friends that I was "just like a little adult." The most devastating words that I could hear were "I'm so disappointed in you" or "I guess you're just not mature enough to handle that." That last one hurt the most. If I had only thought to respond with "Mom, I'm seven!" I might have felt a whole lot better. But instead, I tried my best to be thirty-seven, to be better at being a little adult.

As a result, I didn't have very many friends in school. Not surprisingly, none of the kids in my class wanted to be adulted by me. I was a well-trained Border Collie, and my classmates were not sheep. I would occasionally find one friend with whom I would have a best-friend relationship, but in any sort of a group situation, I was a disaster. I didn't know how to be a kid. My parents and my teachers didn't understand. I had such great conversations with the adults! Why didn't I fit in with other kids? When I was in the second grade, they sent me to the school guidance counselor to find out.

The school guidance counselor put me through a whole battery of tests. Some of the tests had words, some had numbers, and some had shapes. All of them were timed. None of them involved kids or adults or people of any kind. Nevertheless, the guidance counselor arrived at a diagnosis. He called my parents and asked them to come together to a meeting in his office and to bring me. The diagnosis he delivered: I was gifted. Off-the-charts gifted. Gifted kids are awkward with other kids, he assured my parents. It's nothing to be concerned about, he added. With their permission, the school would put me in a special class for gifted kids. My parents were thrilled. Their little adult was gifted! As for me, I had had enough of meetings with the guidance counselor and was just happy to be done with all this testing business and go home.

There were two kinds of kids that got put into the gifted class. There were the kids who were super smart, and there were the kids whose parents did their homework for them. I'm not sure if the school administrators just never caught on, or if they didn't care, or if there was some sort of money or status involved in determining who got put into the gifted class, but it made an awkward situation worse. I didn't fit in any better with those kids – they were still kids, and I was still a confused Border Collie. No problem had been solved for me. Not only was I not learning how to be a kid, I was now also expected to compete academically with many of the other kids' parents. I slogged away and did my best, but with all of those parents as competition, I came in year after year as a middle-of-the pack gifted kid. I was average. And I was still awkward.

Looking back on all this now lends perspective to a few themes that have run through my life. One is a tendency that I have had to try to "adult" others. To be the Border Collie in the relationship. This has not made me a particularly good partner.

Another theme has been an endless pursuit of trying to live up to the little adult that I felt my parents expected me to be. Trying to do everything on my own. Needing to prove that I was all grown up. That I didn't need help or saving or rescuing. This theme has been manifest in my vehement rejection of and feelings of shame around accepting help or even well-intended advice. Accepting help meant that I was immature. Weak. Incapable. A disappointment. A failure. Unworthy of love, from myself or from anyone else.

A third theme has been a craving for intimate interaction. By intimate, I don't necessarily mean physical, although physical intimacy has served as a proxy for the type of intimacy that I have craved. By intimate, I mean the type of interaction where individuals truly get to know one another and trust each other with their dreams, their fears, their desires, and their faults, and support each other as they strive and stumble and continually grow into who they were designed to be.

My parents loved and supported me with all of their hearts, but they never really knew me or let me get to know them. I'm sure that this was partly because they didn't have great role models themselves, and partly because they were simply overwhelmed with their own lives. But I'm also sure that it was partly because they had a lot of fear around what they would learn about me as well as what I would learn about them and what they would learn about themselves and about their own abilities to walk through all of that with me. Walking with me through my insecurities and uncertainties around identity, sexuality, and spirituality, and my associated coping mechanisms of alcohol, avoidance, and intentional ignorance, would risk coming face-to-face with any of these issues that might be less settled in their own lives than they had allowed themselves to admit. It would risk disrupting the balanced relationship of parent-as-perfect-role-model and child-as-pupil that they had so carefully cultivated to keep both me and themselves safe. It was much easier to float blissfully on the surface than it was to acknowledge the messiness of being imperfect humans and to dive into the mess together.

Understanding this has shed light for me on a lifetime of looking for love and intimacy wherever I could find it. I had found intimacy with the spirit of music, but it had failed me. I had found intimacy with God, but a ministry of humans had failed me, and I had laid the blame for their failure at God's feet. I had found no intimacy in marriage or personal relationships, because I had replicated the relationship that I had with my parents and had never ventured beneath the surface. And now that I was back in close connection with my parents, I desperately wanted an intimate relationship with them, as I believe they did with me, but none of us knew how to do it, and we were all too afraid to try. Too afraid to sacrifice the sweet and now short time that we all had together to risk diving into the unknown, messy depths of intimacy.

CHAPTER FOURTEEN

Reciprocity

Several months after I moved to Twain Harte, the contract with my legal client in Florida came to an end. I was not licensed to practice law in California, which meant that work was going to be a problem. The way that bar licenses operate, some states have reciprocity with other states, and some don't. If you are licensed in a state that has reciprocity with one or more other states, you can simply fill out a form, pass a background check, and pay a fee to obtain a license to practice law in any other state that has reciprocity with the state where you are licensed. In 2012 (and still as of this writing), Florida and California each had reciprocity with no one. This left me with two choices: take the California bar exam or look for a different line of work.

I was not at all excited about the idea of taking another bar exam. The mere thought of repeating all that stress made me nauseous. However, the prospects for work in my small, mountain town were limited. The local Walmart, McDonald's, and Starbucks each had entry-level positions available, but that wasn't quite the type of work that I had in mind. I saw an ad posted in the classified section of the town's tiny, local newspaper by a real estate brokerage that was looking to bring on additional agents. Given my background in new home marketing and in real estate law, I was pretty sure I that could figure out how to sell houses. With a little research, I learned that the courses that I had taken for my MBA and for my JD plus my business and legal experience collectively met nearly all the requirements to qualify me to sit for California's real estate broker exam. So I took the remaining few real estate courses online, passed the comparatively easier real estate broker exam, and spent the next year helping folks to buy and sell homes in my small, mountain community.

Going the real estate route proved to be an excellent decision. I worked in a fun office with great agents and a sharp managing broker named Kimberly. I got to know the local neighborhoods, and I had the flexibility to continue to spend lots of time with my parents. Still, something was missing. My evenings with Mom and Dad were heartwarming and light, but I craved something deeper and more intimate. I longed for that elusive, intensely personal relationship that was made just for me. I had a strong sense that I was in the location where I needed to be, but I just didn't have the patience to wait it out. I was a make-it-happen kind of person, not a wait-and-see kind of person. I had a hole in my life, and it was up to me to fill it.

We tend to find what we go looking for, so it wasn't long after I had posted a profile on an online dating site before I had found myself a girlfriend. Having learned a thing or two from my experiences in Florida, I had decided to be more intentional and selective about partnering up this time. I had made a list of non-negotiables: Must have own source of income. No un-mitigated psychoses. No smoking. Alcohol was okay in moderation, but no other drugs of any kind. And very important: Must have been out of previous relationship for at least six months. That last one alone would forestall quite a bit of drama.

After scrolling through dozens of profiles, I came across one that looked promising. This woman was an accomplished professional. She owned her home. She was a former law enforcement officer and had no tolerance for drug use. She didn't smoke. She had no apparent psychoses. And she assured me that she had been single for more than six months. This woman checked all the boxes. We arranged to meet up for a date.

My date lived in Sunnyvale near where my parents had lived when they first married, which was about a two-and-a-half-hour drive west from Twain Harte, so she and I agreed to meet up at one of the gay bars that I had found in the central valley, which was roughly midway between our two towns. I arrived early to secure a table in a section of the bar that wasn't too loud for conversation. When my date came in the door, she looked like her profile photo, which was a good first sign. That didn't always happen in the online dating world. My date wore a huge grin and had brought me a single red rose that she had clipped from her garden. We hit it off immediately, and that became the first of many dates.

After several months of one or the other of us driving back and forth so that we could spend time together, my now-girlfriend and I decided that I would move into her home. From a career perspective, my relocating to Sunnyvale made more sense for both of us than the other way around, and Sunnyvale was still close enough to Twain Harte for me to spend meaningful time with my parents.

Once I got settled in Sunnyvale, I had to address the work situation again. After dabbling briefly in a sales role in financial services, I realized that if I intended to stay in California and wanted to have any kind of a career without starting over again from zero, I really did need a California bar license. So, as unpalatable as the idea was, I went online, bought another set of used bar exam course materials off of ebay – this time tailored for California – and began the daunting task of studying for California's three-day bar exam.

The California bar exam has a reputation for being the most difficult bar exam in the country. This is a myth based on sloppy science and is not supported by relevant facts. The exam was indeed extremely difficult, but it was no more difficult than Florida's. While it is true that California has a much lower pass rate than other states (California's overall pass rate hovers around 50%), it is also true that you can take California's bar exam without ever having gone to law school or even having earned any kind of college degree whatsoever. Two years of college attendance plus working in a law office will suffice. There is also no shortage of unaccredited online "law schools" in California that will happily take your money and sell you a fancy degree to hang on your wall along with the accompanying illusion that you are prepared to take the bar exam.

This inexplicably low exam qualification threshold results in a lot of people sitting for California's bar exam who have no business being in the room. Tragically for them, by the time they realize that they've been grossly underprepared (usually by about question number four), they've spent an awful lot of time and an awful lot of money, and they have very little chance of ever passing the bar exam without going back and getting an academically sound legal education. At this point, either they have to start over or they have to give up. Whichever path they choose, they're still stuck with the bill. This is a racket, and it is sad.

Here's the myth-busting part: If you filter the California bar exam results data to look at just the subset of exam-takers who attended an ABA-accredited law school, you have a true apples-to-apples comparison with other states' statistics. Sifting California's data in this way, the resulting pass rate is similar to the pass rate for many other states' bar exams, and in 2014, it was nearly identical to Florida's.

Armed with this perspective, I took an if-it-ain't-broke-don't-fix-it approach. I studied for California's exam in exactly the same way that I had studied for Florida's exam, for the same amount of time, and I achieved the same result: pass. On the day that exam results were posted, I called my parents to share the news, and they were thrilled. Their little adult had passed the "most difficult bar exam in the country" and would soon be a bona fide California lawyer.

By this time, gay marriage had been legalized in California, and when my girlfriend proposed to me, I said yes. In hindsight, there were a lot of red flags that we both missed. For one, her definition of "out of a relationship" for at least six months was different from mine. There was a whole lot of drama in the first few months involving not one but two of her not-so-exes that did not engender a strong sense of trust in me. For another, we were both take-control kind of people who were used to having to do everything for ourselves, and often for others who relied upon us. If you have ever watched two Border Collie pups trying to herd one another, our relationship looked a lot like that. The intention was well-meaning, but the result was a lot of crossed-up wires and tripping over one another. Gay or otherwise, we simply weren't compatible life partners. But I think that we were both so enamored with the idea of making a life with someone who cared for the other and who was also professionally and psycho-socially stable that we willingly overlooked those red flags. My parents were much less thrilled with this announcement, but they kept me close and continued to love and support me as their daughter despite the fact that they didn't support my decision or my lifestyle.

One spring Saturday morning, my sister happened to be visiting my parents from her home in Arizona. My wife and I were making the drive from Sunnyvale to Twain Harte, and I was looking forward to spending the weekend visiting with my whole family. As we approached a detour that we had planned to take to see the scenic wildflowers that bloom at that time of year, my cell phone rang. It was my sister. Dad was in a bad way. It had come on suddenly. My sister urged us to skip the detour and to drive straight to Twain Harte as quickly as we could.

When I walked into the house, I found my whole little family in my parents' bedroom, and Dad was in bed. He didn't look good. As I approached his bedside, Dad looked up at me and smiled a gentle, peaceful smile. "I waited for you to get here," Dad said softly.

I nodded and took hold of his hand.

"It wasn't easy," he added.

"I know, Dad. I love you."

During the previous few months, Dad had had a couple of strokes and had also taken a pretty serious fall. He had bounced back from each of those, but there would be no more bouncing back now. There was no point in taking him to the hospital. Dad was dying, and he was in the comfortable, familiar, loving surroundings of his own home.

We called two of Dad's pastors to come and visit him that weekend. Dad's longtime friend, Pastor Chuck, came first. Dad had requested Pastor Chuck, and when he got there, they prayed together. The next day, the big, strong, teddy bear of a youth pastor from Dad's church, Pastor Noel, came to visit at my request. Pastor Noel had been nothing but warm, welcoming, and helpful to me personally as well as to my family as I had gotten to know him over the years. Pastor Noel carefully lifted my Dad's frail body up out of the bed and carried him into an adjoining room that had a large, picture window through which, every night, God would paint a new, glorious, multi-colored sunset over the valley below. Pastor Noel laid Dad gently onto the wheeled, hospital-type bed that the local hospice agency had set up in that room so that we could more easily attend to Dad's final needs.

Dad spent a total of three days fading in and out of consciousness over the course of that weekend, looking longingly toward the sky when he was awake, reaching his hands heavenward. And then, on the third evening, he got his final wish. Dad left his cancer-ridden, earthly body peacefully behind and went to be with his Lord.

I have always surmised that the reason that women are designed to live longer than men is so that wives can give their husbands the profoundly unselfish gift of outliving them. Mom was devastated by the loss of her husband of over fifty years. But women are built strong, and even in her grief-stricken state, Mom found the strength not only to push through all the things that needed to be handled when a loved one dies, but also to carry on somehow without Dad. After the service was over and the details had all been handled and the stream of well-wishers had subsided to a slow trickle, every day that Mom went on living on her own was a day that she was giving Dad the gift of never having to live a day without her.

Soon after Dad passed, it became evident to my sister and me that Mom had been giving so much of herself to Dad that none of us had paid much attention to Mom's own decline or to the issues that were going unattended around the house. As we collectively tag-teamed to address those issues – Mom from Twain Harte, me from Sunnyvale, and my sister from Arizona – it began to sink in for all of us that living in my parents' shared retirement home was too much for Mom to manage on her own. Aside from the challenges of keeping up with all of the tasks of day-to-day living on her own, the property itself was simply too high-maintenance for Mom to handle, especially in the winter time, when it was not unusual for snow storms to cause icy and impassible roads and power outages that would last for several days. Our wonderful family friend Larry did his best to help Mom whenever she called, but as her needs became greater and more frequent, it was neither fair to Larry nor safe for Mom for her to continue to live in that house alone.

One of the most lucid things that Dad had said during his final days was spoken to my Mom, my sister, and me all together. Dad had motioned for the three of us to gather close around him. "No matter what happens," Dad instructed us, "you girls stick together." Dad had held each of our gaze, one by one, looking for a nod of confirmation from each of us. He got those nods. Now, it was time for "us girls" to make good on that promise, and my wife was on board.

Knowing that we needed to consolidate the family geographically, Mom, my sister, my wife, and I considered and evaluated where each of us currently lived. Twain Harte was out. There was no real prospect of work for my sister, my wife, or me there. Sunnyvale was also out. Moving to the San Francisco Bay area in 2016 was simply not a financially affordable prospect for Mom. Heck, it was barely affordable for my wife's and my two-income household. That left Arizona. A state whose bar has reciprocity with every state that has reciprocity with it. Which included neither of the two states where I was currently licensed to practice law.

CHAPTER FIFTEEN

The Innovation Challenge

Arizona is hot! At least the Phoenix area is, in summer. When I pulled the moving truck and car carrier alongside the curb in front of our new home in Mesa, Arizona, in June of 2016, I opened up the driver's-side door and was hit by a blast of air so hot and so dry that I immediately closed the door in shock and reevaluated the wisdom of this whole decision. *How do people live here?! This is not even safe!* When some family in a wagon train was traveling westward across the North American continent in the mid-1800s, what kind of man looked around at all these rocks and sand and dust and cacti and scorpions and snakes and said to his wife, "This is it, honey! Unload the wagons. Let's live here!" I seriously contemplated turning the whole rig around on the spot and driving back to where I had just come from. But the house in California was sold, and this one was bought, so I opened the door back up and ventured out into the furnace.

Mom had arrived in Arizona a month earlier, and my sister and our family friend Larry had helped Mom to move into a small house of her own about a mile from my sister's house, which was about a twenty-minute drive from where my wife and I now lived. Mom enjoyed the privacy and autonomy of living in her own home, but my wife and I had intentionally purchased a home with plenty of extra room in anticipation of a time when either one or both of our mothers might not be able to live independently. For the time being, though, the three-home arrangement worked well, and "us girls" enjoyed many evenings and weekends swimming in each other's pools, drinking iced tea, wine, and cocktails, playing cards, and watching *Wheel of Fortune* and *Jeopardy!* on TV.

At the time when we all had made the decision to consolidate the family in Arizona, I had been working for an estate planning law firm in San Francisco. Traffic in the San Francisco Bay area was brutal, so rather than make the drive each day, I would ride the commuter train from Sunnyvale to San Francisco and back. The ride was an hour and a half each way, and I initially used that time to work, to catch up on the day's news, or simply to unwind on the ride home. Once the decision had been made to move to Arizona, I used my train time to update my résumé, to apply for jobs in the Phoenix area, and to study for the Arizona bar exam. Because I had taken California's bar exam relatively recently, not all of that material had yet leaked out of my brain, so the studying went a little bit easier this time, but it was nerve-racking all the same.

Before exam results had been posted, I received a job offer from a leading financial services company that had a large corporate footprint in Phoenix. The position that I was offered gave strong preference to candidates with a law degree, but it did not require an Arizona bar license. The role involved reviewing clients' estate planning documents, helping those clients and their advisers to understand how their plans would play out, and suggesting planning opportunities that those clients might want to consider. It was solidly in my wheelhouse of experience and expertise.

The position also offered me the flexibility of working four ten-hour days per week so that I could spend every Wednesday with Mom. And, surprisingly, the salary was better than what I had been earning as an attorney in San Francisco. Both of these things would be hard to beat.

I accepted the offer. I later learned that I had passed the Arizona bar exam, but by that time, I had a bird in the hand, and it was a good opportunity. So, I held onto that bird, and I started my new job as a wealth strategist in financial services on the Monday after I arrived in Arizona.

Hiring into a publicly traded, Fortune 500 company opened up a whole new world for me. Up to this time, I had never worked for an organization with even a hundred employees. This company not only had tens of thousands of employees, but it also had locations throughout the country as well as internationally. It had departments and divisions and nearly every kind of job that a person could think of, all within a corporate eco-system which itself resided within a whole industry made up of companies with similar types of opportunities. This was an environment in which I could grow, and maybe even shine.

From the first week of new employee orientation, I became a student of the company. I wanted to understand everything about how a company of that size and complexity worked. I started with my own job, learning its place within my department, my department's place within the division, and the division's place within the company. I studied the company's annual report, its financials, its regulatory filings, the demographics of its clients, the positioning of its products, its competitive landscape, and the market and economic trends that drove the company's strategy. The MBA classes that I had taken so many years ago were finally coming in handy!

The more that I learned, the more that I became intrigued by what I perceived to be a gap in the company's strategy. Like a puzzle with a missing piece, it reminded me of the tests with the shapes and the numbers and the words that I had taken in the school guidance counselor's office. Tapping into my legal knowledge and my entrepreneurial antennae, I came up with an idea for a type of product that could help to fill that gap. However, I was a brand-new employee in an individual contributor role in a small department. Who was I to pitch such an idea, and who would even take that meeting?

No sooner had I asked myself those questions than an opportunity came along. I arrived at work one morning to find an email in my inbox announcing the company's annual Innovation Challenge. This was a competition sponsored by our business segment's executive leadership team each year to elevate and fund employee ideas that could benefit the whole company. Any employee could post an idea electronically to an internal website where everyone in the company could then vote for their favorites. Individuals and teams who submitted the ideas that received the most votes would have the opportunity to pitch their ideas in person to the leadership team, which had budget available to allocate toward implementing the winning idea. This was my shot! I wanted to win that challenge, but more importantly, I wanted to get my product idea in front of that leadership team.

One of the things that I had learned as I had studied the company was that this was a place where nobody did anything alone. Lone rangers had no voice. In fact, they were frowned-upon. One of the cultural tenets that had been drilled into us at the new employee orientation was that of teamwork. In a company of this size, whatever you needed, there was surely someone here who had expertise in that area. In a publicly-traded company where running lean is closely-watched as a significant driver of shareholder wealth, there was little tolerance for re-inventing the human wheel when the company warehouse of talent was stacked full of every kind of wheel imaginable.

I knew that I had zero chance of putting together a winning Innovation Challenge proposal on my own. But I was so new to the company that I didn't even know how to begin to pull a team together. So, I took my idea to my leader. My leader's name was Corey, and Corey was the manager who had hired me into my role in the company. Corey was smart, personable, a strong leader, and a gifted and supportive developer of talent. Corey had recognized my aspirations from day one, and he was eager to support me in making the needed connections to pitch my idea to the executive leadership team.

Corey suggested that I partner with another wealth strategist named Jay who had recently floated a related idea in a departmental team meeting and who was well-connected within the company. Jay welcomed the idea, and together, we enlisted the assistance of various experts serving in strategically relevant functions throughout the company to assemble a well-researched, well-supported, and visually attractive proposal. We then reached out to everyone in the company that each of us knew, personally pitched our idea to them, and invited them to vote for our idea and to share our proposal with their own colleagues. We sent out daily email blasts reminding our idea's supporters to vote. The strategy worked! Jay's and my team was one of ten finalists who were invited to fly to corporate headquarters to pitch our idea in person to the leadership team.

As a brand new "nobody" in a company with tens of thousands of employees, getting in front of a leadership team at that level was a tremendous opportunity for me. The product that Jay and I pitched was a little too rich for the budget that was allocated to fund the winning Innovation Challenge idea, but our presentation was well received by the leadership team. More importantly for me, the whole exercise of entering the challenge, promoting our idea company-wide through grass-roots channels, gaining sponsorship, and presenting our idea to key executive leaders provided tremendous visibility for me and opened doors to maneuver within the company that otherwise would have taken years to develop. It was a fast track to becoming a "somebody" in my new career world of corporate financial services.

A few months after the Innovation Challenge, I was back at my desk in Phoenix, documenting notes from my last call of the afternoon before wrapping up my day as a wealth strategist and heading home. All of my colleagues had already left, and the office was quiet. Suddenly, the vice president for our division appeared in my doorway. She strode right in and sat down on the return end of my C-shaped desk.

"Hi! How was your day?" she inquired, dangling her feet casually from her perch on my desk.

This was unusual. My meetings with this vice president had mostly been large, formal meetings. She and I had also attended some of the same company events and were acquainted with one another, but I couldn't recall her ever stopping by to visit me in the office.

"It was a good day," I responded, and I briefly recounted a particularly successful meeting from that day with one of the division's advisers and his clients.

"How do you like working as a wealth strategist?" her inquiry continued.

"I like it," I answered, adding how much I enjoyed collaborating with my colleagues, and heaping well-deserved praise on my team leader, Corey.

"Mmm hmm." She paused. And then, "How would you like to come work for me?"

Ah-hah! That's why she was here. Thanks to my research of the company, I understood everything that was embedded in that question. All of this vice president's direct reports were leaders. She was asking me if I would like to lead a team of portfolio advisers and financial planners.

"I'd love to!" I responded without hesitation. "As long as it's alright with Corey."

She could see that I had understood. "It will be alright with Corey," she assured me with a smile.

"Then let's do it!"

She stood up. "You'll have to get your CFP," she added, "and a couple more securities licenses."

"Okay," I said.

And with that, she walked back to her office, and I had a new job to prepare for – and another round of tests to take.

Securities licensing exams had always been fairly routine undertakings for me, but the Certified Financial Planner exam was going to be a bit of a project. Qualifying to take the CFP exam turned out to be an even simpler process for me than qualifying to take the California

Real Estate Broker exam had been. My MBA and JD classes plus my business and legal experience fulfilled all but one of the requirements to sit for the CFP exam. I would need to submit a sample financial plan, but other than that, there was nothing more that I needed to do other than to apply. Taking and passing the CFP exam, however, was going to be another story.

By now, I had the exam-taking drill down pat: go online, buy books, study books, take test. I felt like Bill Murray in the movie, *Groundhog Day*. Equally déjà vu, all my colleagues were aghast that I didn't enroll in the commercial test prep course for this exam. The company would pay for the course. Nobody took the CFP exam without sitting for weeks on end in the over-air-conditioned hotel ballroom watching disembodied heads reading review material aloud on video. It was a rite of passage! I was crazy to turn that down, everyone advised. As was my habit, I tuned out the nay-sayers, preferring to stick with my tried-and-true method – if it ain't broke, don't fix it.

When my ebay box full of used exam prep books arrived, I sliced through the packaging tape, grabbed the first book off the top of the pile, fixed myself a cocktail, walked out to my backyard, and stretched out on a chaise lounge next to the pool to begin to read. I didn't have to flip through very many pages before it became painfully apparent that I had bitten off much more than I had imagined. This exam was going to be a whole lot harder than the California Real Estate Broker exam or the securities licensing exams had been. The CFP exam wasn't just going to be hard, it was going to be bar exam hard. What on earth had I said yes to?

By this time, I was already immersed in my new job, leading a team of portfolio advisers and financial planners. Keeping that job was contingent upon my obtaining the CFP designation in short order, and my prior job had already been filled. I was just going to have to suck it up and study for another really hard test. I knew that the opportunity would be worth the effort in the long run, but I made a mental note-to-self to stop choosing career paths that required me to take really hard tests!

CHAPTER SIXTEEN

The Absence of Life

When I started my new role, I was warmly welcomed by the team of portfolio advisers and financial planners that I had been tapped to lead. I was grateful for that. I had already had the opportunity to work with many of them on a peer-to-peer level, helping their clients with estate planning matters. Shifting from a peer-level relationship to a supervisor/employee relationship can often be tricky, but my team was comprised of seasoned professionals and all-around quality folks, and every one of them welcomed me with open arms.

During my second week on the job, I celebrated my fiftieth birthday. I arrived at the office that day to find balloons, neatly wrapped gifts, and a wonderful birthday card containing a hand-written message from each person on my team. Shortly after lunch, everyone huddled around one team member's desk, and my team motioned for me to come over. Another team member proudly displayed a birthday cake that she had baked and decorated herself. Someone lit the candles, and the team was just getting ready to sing happy birthday to me when my wife appeared.

My wife had been hired into the company shortly after I was. She worked in a different department on a different floor, so we rarely saw one another during the day, but we would commute back and forth together, taking advantage of the carpool lane on the freeways and the preferred carpool parking in the company lot. I thought it was really sweet that my team had invited my wife upstairs to celebrate my birthday and to enjoy a slice of cake with us.

"I've been looking for you!" my wife huffed breathlessly as she walked up to me. "We have to go."

I was puzzled. It was early afternoon, much too early to be leaving for the day.

"The team made me a cake!" I exclaimed, brushing off my wife's statement. "Have a piece with us!"

"We have to go right now," my wife insisted.

I didn't understand. Clearly, my team was celebrating my birthday. What could possibly be so urgent that it couldn't wait a few minutes? I was a little annoyed at my wife's lack of perception of the situation.

"Your sister has been texting us," my wife persisted. "I've been texting you, too. Did you not see our messages?" My wife and I had very different phone styles. I tended to set my phone aside when I was in the company of others. This had the benefit of allowing me to be intentionally present, but it was frustrating to my wife when she was trying to reach me with any urgency. My wife and I also had differing definitions of what was urgent, which only added to our mutual frustration.

"I didn't," I conceded with poorly masked exasperation, "but we're doing my birthday right now. Can we just have some cake first? The team made a nice celebration for me. Look!" I beamed, pointing to the homemade cake and the flames dancing atop the colorful candles. I had found a role where I excelled, and I was leading a team of people who supported and believed in me. My team had gone to no small amount of effort to make me feel appreciated, even loved. I was not about to be herded away from that moment, in the middle of my own birthday celebration, for somebody else's agenda of questionable urgency. My wife could wait a few minutes. I was going to enjoy this moment, and she was not going to ruin it.

"No! We have to go *now*. Your mom's in the hospital."

The words hit me like a sailboat boom swinging around on a hard jibe, instantly knocking all the wind from my sails. My wife and my sister had been trying to get my attention about an actual emergency, and I was too wrapped up in my own agenda to hear them. They needed me. Mom needed me. My wife was right. We had to go now. I expressed my apologies to the team, left the cake and the melting candles and the birthday celebration behind, and hustled with my wife out to the car.

As we sped down the freeway, all of my feelings about my birthday and the interruption and my differences with my wife and even my fear for Mom's situation fell away. I was operating on instinct now, emotionless. I don't know why I was in such a hurry to get to the hospital. I knew. My sister hadn't said so in her texts, but I knew. Mom had died. It was already over. That was a fact, and it wasn't going to be any more or less true based on how fast I drove. I felt oddly calm. Not peaceful, just calm, like I was suspended in space and time.

When my wife and I walked up to the front desk in the ER and I asked where we could find Mom, we were directed to a small room where we found my sister, sitting alone. No Mom, no bed, no doctor, no hospital-looking trappings of any sort, just my sister in a chair with a couple of empty chairs next to her and a coffee table in the middle of the room and a few more chairs lined up along the wall opposite where my sister was sitting. My sister stood up, she and I gave each other a knowing look, and we embraced.

Neither my sister nor I have ever been a panic-in-the-moment type of person. If there is ever an emergency or a crisis of any kind, you want my sister or me around. We assess the situation, we triage, and we take care of business. The more harrowing the situation, the more calm and more take-charge we become. Only after the crisis is over and everyone else's needs have been attended to and we are in the solitude of our own homes do we process whatever emotion comes along with the thing that just happened.

My sister explained that she had found Mom unconscious in her home after having just spoken with her minutes earlier by phone. My sister had called 911 and had followed all of the resuscitation instructions given to her by the operator via speaker phone until the paramedics arrived and took over. There was a brief moment in the hospital where the doctors were able to regain a weak pulse, but it didn't last. Mom was gone.

My wife, my sister, and I all sat quietly in the room where we had been instructed to remain, waiting for someone from the hospital to come in to give us next steps. While we waited, my sister shared more about what had happened. About how Mom had been waiting to be picked up by an Uber that my sister had ordered for her so that Mom could go and get her nails done. About how my sister had called the Uber driver when she noticed that he had been stopped at Mom's house for too long. About how the Uber driver had told my sister that Mom wasn't answering the door. About how my sister had dismissed the Uber driver and had driven over to Mom's house herself. About how my sister had known, the moment that the Uber driver had told her that Mom wasn't answering the door. Just like I had known on the drive to the hospital.

Eventually, someone showed up to the room where we were waiting. But instead of the hospital staff member that we had been expecting, a police officer entered the room. The police officer sat down in a chair across from the three of us. She had concerns. My sister hadn't cried during the 911 call. She hadn't cried when the doctor told her that Mom had died. She wasn't crying now. Neither was I. Mom hadn't been morbidly ill. There was no obvious cause of death. Also, Mom had a cast on her arm, the result of a fall that she had taken a few weeks prior. Was there anything going on in this situation that we thought the police should be aware of? The officer interviewed the three of us. More cops searched Mom's house. Eventually, absent any indication of unnatural causes, they checked the "heart attack" box on the cause of death form and closed the case.

If there had been a "broken heart" box on the cause of death form, they should have checked that. Mom's and Dad's marriage had been no more perfect than anyone else's, but they had loved each other dearly and had been inseparable since the day that they had met. I still remember vividly every year of my childhood during deer season when my Dad would take a "guys' trip" deep into the wilderness for ten days or so. After several hours of packing out on horseback at the end of the trip, Dad would drive straight home, skipping the showers at the pack station so that he could get back home to Mom. When Dad got out of the car, we could smell him coming before he even got to the house, and he would be so covered from head to toe with sweat and dirt and dust that he was barely recognizable as human. It didn't matter to Mom. She would throw her arms around Dad as if he had just come back from years away at war, and she would want to hear all about every detail of his trip, right then and there.

After Dad got sick, and especially after his strokes, Mom did a yeoman's job of taking care of him, attending to his every need. Towards the end, it was a round-the-clock job. But it was a labor of love for Mom, and it gave her purpose. Then one day, suddenly and all at once, all of that purpose was gone. It wasn't so much Dad's death that had been hard on Mom, it was the absence of Dad's life. Mom loved God and spent a lot of time in prayer, and she continued to be intentional about being a blessing to everyone that she encountered, every day. But the hole that Dad's absence had left in her heart and in her life was just too big to be filled. In the end, Mom had simply crawled into that hole with him.

After the police officer left the room, I was finally permitted to see Mom. A nurse led me down the hall to the hospital room where Mom was, and the nurse allowed me to have a few minutes alone with Mom. Mom was covered with a blanket up to her shoulders. I was glad. Mom hated to be cold. Her eyes were closed. She looked peaceful. I stood quietly by her side.

In the year since we had consolidated the family in Arizona, Mom had been struggling more and more to live independently. We all had recently conceded that the time had come for Mom to move into my wife's and my home. The move had been planned for the upcoming weekend. I knew that Mom was not looking forward to giving up her independence, and that she struggled with the idea of sharing a living environment with a relationship that she did not condone. The move would have been hard on her. It would have been hard on all of us. I was glad for Mom that she didn't have to go through that. Mom's last moments of conscious life had been spent in her own home, just as Dad's had been. I leaned over and kissed Mom on the forehead and told her that I loved her, and then I turned and walked out of the room, utterly lost.

You don't truly realize just how much a part of your life that someone is until they're not there anymore. When Dad had died, I had really struggled with his absence. Especially as my sister and I took on more and more responsibility with Mom, I would often find myself driving down the road in tears, crying out to my father. "Dad, where are you?" I would wail. "Where ARE you? You're supposed to be here! Come back!" Dad was always the one with all the answers. No matter the situation, he would always know what to do. With him gone, I felt like I didn't have anybody to ask anymore.

Now that Mom was gone too, I felt completely adrift. No matter what had happened in my life, I could always count on Mom to be there for me. To be proud of me. I could call Mom any time with the most inconsequential news of the smallest little thing that had gone right in my life, and you would think that I had just brokered world peace. "Oh, Honey, that is HUGE!" she would exclaim. And she meant it. She was really proud of my sister and me. Now that Mom was gone, who was going to be proud of me?

———————

A few days after Mom died, I was going through her wallet, attending to all of the things that need to be done when someone passes away. Tucked into a pocket of its own was a well-worn slip of paper on which were printed the following words:

My Daily Commitment

Today, dear God, I am available. Please make me usable and help me to be Christ to my family, to someone in need, and to every life I touch this day.

These words were not just ink on a forgotten scrap of paper. This was how Mom lived her life, every day. I tucked that slip of paper into my own wallet, and it remains there to this day.

CHAPTER SEVENTEEN

Catch-Up

My sister was born Judith, but throughout our childhood, everyone called her Judy. At some point during her teenage years, she announced that she preferred the spelling, "Judie." From that day forward, Judie it was. Like me, Judie had been the target of teasing as a child. Unlike me, Judie had overcome that station and had moved up in the pecking order of schoolchildren by the time that she reached high school. During her early teens, Judie had met a friend who showed her how to walk and talk and dress and fix her hair and wear her makeup in order to fit in with the popular kids. In high school, Judie and that same friend had both tried out for the cheerleading squad, and they had both made it. They had tons of friends and almost as many boyfriends, and they were involved in all manner of activities and parties outside of school day and night.

Actually attending school was another matter. Judie is extremely smart, so she didn't need teachers to repeat information to her eight or nine times before it sank in. When Judie heard it, she got it, and then she was bored. Judie is also a problem-solver, and she detests inefficiency. Daily attendance at school was a waste of time for her, and there was no shortage of interesting things to do outside of school. So, she problem-solved. Judie showed up at school just often enough to get the gist of what was going on in class, and then she spent the rest of her time with her friends getting into all kinds of non-school-related activities during most school days.

This resulted in more than a few phone calls from the school to our home. By the time that Judie and I were in high school, the daytime family had grown up and disbanded, and Mom had taken a school secretary job in a different district from where Judie and I were enrolled. Consequently, when the phone would ring during the afternoon, neither of my parents would be home. Judie was usually about as far away from home as she could get without actually moving out. That left me.

Whenever the phone would ring, I would drop whatever I was doing and race to the kitchen to answer it. This was in the days when phones were still attached to the wall, and the handset was still attached to the phone with a long spiral cord that always seemed to be hopelessly tangled up. This was also in the days before answering machines, which themselves were the predecessor to voice mail, so if the phone rang and you didn't get to it in time to lift the handset from its cradle before the phone stopped ringing, there would be no way to know who had called. You would just have to wait for the person to call back. That was a bad option in this situation. I needed to be the one to answer the phone whenever someone from the school called.

"Simpson residence," I would answer matter-of-factly, trying to sound grown-up and not all out of breath from running to the phone. This was how Judie and I were taught to answer the phone so that the caller would know that they had reached the right number. These were the days of rotary phones. To make a phone call, you would stick your finger into the hole in a dial that corresponded to a specific single-digit number, and then you would rotate the dial around clockwise using your finger until your finger hit a metal stop. You would repeat this motion for each numerical digit until you had dialed a whole phone number. It was not unusual to end up calling the wrong number if your dialing was a little sloppy. If the person answering the phone said only "hello," you could get pretty far into the conversation before you realized that you had misdialed and that you were talking to the wrong person.

"Hello, is this Mrs. Simpson?" the voice on the other end of the call would ask. That's when I knew that it was someone from the school. Everyone who knew our family knew that Mom was working and would not be home in the middle of the afternoon, so they wouldn't call her at that time of day. If the call had been a sales call, the caller would have asked for the generic "lady of the house," not for Mom by name.

"Who's calling?" I would ask anyway, just to be sure. My sister and I had been instructed to do this as well. In those days, there was also no caller ID. As horrifying as it sounds to us today, as late as the 1980s, whenever the phone rang, you would just go right ahead and answer it without having any idea of who was on the other end of the line.

"This is so-and-so from the high school," the caller would say, forgetting all about the fact that they had just asked me whether I was Mrs. Simpson. "Your daughter isn't in school today, and we were just calling to check on her and see if she's okay."

"Oh yes," I would answer truthfully. "Judie just wasn't feeling up to coming to school today," also true. "She'll be back in school as soon as she's feeling better." That was a bit more iffy, but not an outright lie, I reasoned to myself.

"Oh, okay, well, I see that she's been missing a lot of school," the caller would usually say.

"We'll make sure that she keeps her grades up," I would answer, knowing that between my parents and my sister herself, they would do just that.

"Okay, well, we hope that, uh, Judith is feeling better soon," the caller would say, reading my sister's formal name from some kind of list or file. The call would then end with thank-yous and goodbyes.

Judie's and my worlds didn't intersect much during our teenage years. We were each navigating adolescence in our own way – me by insulating myself in my safe world of music and trying to be the "good child," and Judie by railing against being in anybody's shadow by blazing her own, opposite path as the "bad child," defiantly rebelling against anything and everything that smacked of authority. But I think that somewhere in the back of our minds, we both must have known that our relationship as sisters was important. While we had almost no interests in common, we had this one little conspiracy going for us that only we knew about. This was probably the single point of connection most responsible for laying the foundation for the close sister-bond that Judie and I share today.

Much to the school truancy administrator's surprise, Judie graduated from high school right on time, and she never looked back. While she retained several of her closest friendships, she broke out of the cultural microcosm of high school popularity and quickly set to work developing a career as a successful business woman. Judie bought her first house in her early twenties, and she was already out-earning my father before she turned thirty. Since then, she has continued to grow her career as a top performing sales leader, assuming greater and greater corporate leadership responsibility over the years.

It was against this backdrop that I had been struggling to build a career of my own that I hoped would make my parents proud. I had passionately loved my time as a musician, but music at that level was not the kind of career that comes with a big salary and a bonus plan and a 401(k). When I had taken a different tack and chosen to pursue a life of service in a ministry that I knew my parents didn't approve of, that had backfired badly, leaving me with a great deal of shame that I had been crawling my way back from ever since.

With both of my parents now gone, I vowed to myself to leverage my credentials and every opportunity that came my way to try to build a professional legacy that my parents would be proud of. Without being conscious of it, I set out to play an impossible game of catch-up with my younger sister, a game that she wasn't playing and wasn't even aware of, for an audience of no one.

The game started off pretty well. In my first year of leading a team of portfolio advisers and financial planners, my team's sales numbers turned around from the worst performing team in our location to the top performing team. Turnover was low, morale was high, and I was getting more and more visibility in the company. The next year went equally well. My team again blew the lid off of its sales goals, and as a leader, I had one of the highest employee engagement scores in the division.

It was at this point that I began to get an education in corporate politics. Not everyone was as happy as I was that my team was doing so well. Not everyone was thrilled that an unlikely turnaround had been led by a team leader with short tenure in the company who had zero prior experience in either portfolio advice or financial planning.

One day, I walked into a leaders meeting to learn that our teams were being reshuffled. Some of my top advisers were being moved to another team, and a number of advisers from that team were being moved to mine. Taking in the advisers from the other team didn't bother me. Helping motivated people to develop professionally has always brought me great joy, especially when I get to be a part of someone's comeback story. But I wasn't too happy with not having been consulted about the shuffle.

My education in corporate politics continued. Newly hired talent that I had personally recruited and interviewed ended up getting assigned to someone else's team. Promotions of my team members that had widely been considered a slam-dunk were denied so that those promotion slots could be allocated elsewhere. When opportunities opened up to advance to the next level of leadership, while I was too early in my own role to make that move, the cream definitely did not rise to the top. It became evident that if I wanted to continue my career development progress, my next move would need to be outside of that part of the organization.

This is where the Innovation Challenge from my first few months at the company really paid off for me. The product idea that Jay and I had pitched to the leadership team had not died with the Innovation Challenge. A small, cross-functional, product development team had been assigned to follow-up on Jay's and my research and do a feasibility study. I was on that team, along with two of the leaders from our company's wholly-owned trust company. If the product were going to be implemented, the trust company was where the product would live.

After one of our product development meetings, I reached out to the more senior of the two trust company leaders and requested a few minutes of his time to discuss a shared concern that we both had expressed during the meeting. The trust company was located in Nevada, so we scheduled a time to meet by phone. We spent most of the meeting working out a strategy to address our shared concern. But before the meeting was over, I made sure to let him know that if the product were ever to get implemented and if the trust company needed someone to lead the effort to stand it up, I would be happy to take that on.

The trust company leader had another, more immediate idea. They had been looking for a new director to lead the trust company's business development function, but they hadn't found quite the right person. He had thought of me, but he had dismissed the thought because he had assumed that I would not be willing to relocate to Nevada. However, since I had brought up the idea of joining the trust company myself, he wondered if I might be interested in the role after all. I told him that I would love to know more about it, so he emailed me the job description, and he said that if I were still interested after I read it, then I should call him back the next day.

I read the job description as soon as we hung up the phone. I was *very* interested. It was a next-level leadership opportunity for me that would use many of the tools in my toolbox – legal knowledge, business strategy, sales and marketing skills, and my favorite: people leadership. I could not have asked for a better next step in my career. Except that the job was located in Nevada.

There were three possible scenarios that I could see playing out in this situation. One would be for my wife and me to move to Nevada. The second would be for me to commute to Nevada each week and return home to Arizona on weekends. The third would be for me to turn the job down. I did not consider a fourth scenario where I would not be offered the job. I knew in my gut that the job was mine.

Of the three possible scenarios, the third, turning the job down, was the only one that would keep what was left of my family together full-time. While there wasn't the same need to remain geographically consolidated now as there had been when Mom was alive, my wife and I had made our home in Arizona. My wife had a good job there. She had become close friends with Judie, and the two of them would golf together on their own or with others at least once a week. The three of us would also have dinner together at least once a week. My sister and I didn't have our parents anymore, but we had each other. Scenario three, turning the job down, would leave all of that undisturbed.

Given these facts, I didn't see scenario number one of my wife and me pulling up roots and moving to Nevada as a real possibility. As for scenario number two, commuting, some groundwork had previously been laid for that. When my wife and I had first married, she had just completed a contract work engagement and was searching for the right next role for herself. We had discussed at that time that if either of us were to find an otherwise perfect role, but one that would require us to work in two different cities, we would be supportive of the other pursuing that role. We had good friends who had done the two-city-shuffle for a few years, and their marriage was stronger for it. For the right opportunity, we would make it work, too.

The conversation had come up again when we had first moved to Arizona and my wife's job search had taken a bit longer than mine. We had examined the possibility of a two-city solution again, and we had reaffirmed our prior agreement that we would be supportive of one another's career decisions if we needed to work in separate cities. However, both of those conversations had been hypothetical, and both times, we had been talking about my wife working in a different city, not me. How would the conversation go now, several years later, when we would be considering an actual real opportunity, and when I would be the one who was looking at a job in a different city?

CHAPTER EIGHTEEN

Mistrust

All of my life, I had been struggling to excel in something. I was never the most athletic kid. I had been average in the gifted class. I had gone from an outstanding trombone player to an ordinary-sounding one. I had had the privilege of performing with some virtuosic singers, but I myself had been just an okay singer. My budding ministry had begun to blossom, but that situation had abruptly withered. The one thing that I did have going for me, though, was that I had well-developed professional communication skills. This had propelled my success both in business and in law. But professional communication is one thing. Personal communication is another thing entirely. I have never tried so hard nor failed so miserably at figuring out how to communicate with anyone than I did in my marriage to my wife.

My wife and I were built very differently. My wife was a planner. I was, and largely still am, the opposite of a planner. I am a just-go-for-it-and-figure-it-out-as-you-go kind of person. The kind of person who drives planners nuts. Not being a planner doesn't mean that I don't do research. For big decisions especially, I do copious amounts of research. But then, after I've reviewed all of the research, I throw it all out the window, and I go with my gut. This is different from taking a calculated risk, because the calculation part for me, if it is present at all, is more back-of-the-napkin than it is spreadsheet analytics. I like to call this method "informed gut." Planners like to call it reckless. There are elements of truth in both statements.

In my wife's and my early years, when I would present an idea to her for discussion, my thoughts would tend to be fairly abstract and high-level. I would typically be met with a request for more information, for better data from which to make a calculated decision. Having learned to anticipate this, I made an effort to do more homework before presenting ideas to her. I would come to these conversations brimming with research and data and facts, hoping that this would facilitate a more productive conversation.

One such idea that I wanted us to consider was moving from our current neighborhood near where my sister lived to a neighborhood closer to where my wife and I both worked. Our bumper-to-bumper commute at the time had been consuming at total of two hours every weekday. With Mom now gone, we had more flexibility in our living arrangement. Rather than coming to my wife with just that raw idea, I set out to do some homework first to make sure that there were indeed homes in our price range in decent neighborhoods near the office. If there weren't, then there would be no point in raising the topic. I poked around online, and the idea indeed appeared promising. So far, so good.

My first mistake in this process was reaching out to our real estate agent on my own. I had seen one house that looked attractive, and I asked our agent what she thought of the house and the neighborhood. Our agent liked the neighborhood, but she let me know that there was already an offer on the house, although it hadn't yet been accepted. If we were interested, we should see the house right away. The problem with this was that my wife was out of town for a couple of days. Here is where I made my second mistake. I arranged to meet our real estate agent at the property. I figured that if I liked it, our agent could let the seller's agent know that there might be a second offer coming in hopes that they might stall on their current offer until I could come back with my wife.

I did like the property, so when my wife returned home, I presented my idea to her immediately and asked if she would like to go and see the house. I had anticipated that she would be pleased that I had done some homework in advance this time. Instead, I was met with anger and mistrust. I had left my wife out of my conversations with the agent and had gone to see the house without her even knowing about it. I could have at least told her what was happening over the phone. To my wife, what I had done didn't feel like homework, it felt sneaky. In my attempts to avoid a conversation where I would have been told that my efforts were not enough, I had simply avoided conversation altogether.

Moving forward, I endeavored to find the right balance of gathering enough information ahead of time to have productive conversations with my wife without going too far in gathering information on my own that she would have wanted to participate in from the beginning. I never did succeed in striking that balance. I couldn't get out of the way of my own fear of being found inadequate. So I just kept screwing up, and the more I screwed up, the more my wife's trust in me eroded.

That was the hardest part for me – the mistrust. I was already losing confidence in the one remaining skill that had been serving me well: communication. But that was just a skill. It was something that could be further developed. I could handle that. My wife's mistrust of me wasn't about a skill, it was about my character. That hurt. Even when I had gotten everything all wrong, I had always been trying to do right. I don't know what agenda my wife thought I was up to that was nefarious. I will never know. But that mistrust hit hard, and before long I was afraid to propose anything anymore.

———

After reading the job description for the role at the trust company, I knew that I had to have the conversation with my wife that same night. I was gripped with anxiety. How had this opportunity even come up in conversation without me running it by my wife in advance?

I should have discussed it with her before I even reached out to the trust company leader. But wait – I had only intended to plant a seed about a hypothetical situation in the future. It was the trust company leader who had countered with the present opportunity. I hadn't gone looking for it. I hadn't had any intention of discussing something this significant with someone else without discussing it with my wife first. It had just come up. I hadn't done anything untrustworthy, had I? I was terrified that I might have somehow blown it again in some way that I didn't even understand or intend. I had no confidence at all going into this conversation. But it had to be had, that much I knew. Waiting and doing more research first was not an option.

At dinnertime that evening, there was nothing to be gained by procrastinating until the end of the meal, so I just went for it. I described the day's events exactly as they had happened. Just the facts, no elaboration or embellishment of any kind. I showed my wife the printed-out job description so that she could read it for herself, rather than relying on my interpretation. I presented what I thought were the three possible scenarios, and I laid out my thoughts about the pros and cons of each. I reminded my wife of our prior discussions. I told her that I really wanted this job, and I explained from my heart what it would mean to me. I also told her that I was committed to our marriage, that it was the priority, and that I would understand and respect if she couldn't support my taking this job, if she thought that the circumstances were different now from what we had discussed before. And then I held my breath and braced for impact.

To my utter astonishment, the conversation went well. It was respectful and productive. We talked about all of the pros and cons. As I suspected, we dismissed scenario number one. My wife was not interested in moving to Nevada. We telephoned our friends who had done the two-city shuffle themselves. They knew my wife better than they knew me, but they believed that we could handle it. After that call and a bit more discussion, my wife told me that she was supportive of me continuing to pursue the opportunity, understanding that if it came to fruition, it would mean me commuting back and forth to Nevada.

"Are you sure?" I asked.

"Yes, I'm sure."

I arrived at work the next morning to find that the wheels had already been set in motion. Apparently, the trust company leadership was pretty excited about the idea of me joining their team, and the president of the trust company had socialized the idea with my current leader overnight, before my wife and I had even agreed that I would pursue the job. That mistimed sequence of events ruffled a few feathers at the office, but we got it all smoothed out, and the next thing you know, I was moving one car, all of my work clothes, and a second set of toiletries to a small, furnished apartment in Henderson, Nevada, just outside of Las Vegas.

Career-wise, the trust company move turned out to be an excellent decision. I had the privilege of working directly for the president of the trust company. His name was Braden, and Braden was hands down the best business leader that I have ever had. Braden challenged me to grow, and he gave me the resources, the responsibility, and the room to maneuver that I needed in order to do so. I loved my colleagues and my team, too, and I had another opportunity to turn a low-engagement, low-performance situation into a resounding success story. During my years with the trust company, I learned more about business strategy and corporate political strategy from Braden than I have learned from every other business leader that I've ever had, combined. The entire experience was a tremendous confidence-booster for me, and I loved that job.

Personally, however, the two-city shuffle was rough. It didn't help that a summer monsoon flooded the lower level of our home during my first week on the job, which left my wife to deal with the mess and the clean-up and the insurance company and the contractors on her own. It also didn't help that the level of responsibility of my new job involved me doing some work on weekends and staying abreast of email while on vacation, both of which chipped away at time that was supposed to be reserved for my wife and me to spend together. My wife was understandably frustrated.

But where things really fell apart was when I proposed an idea to save us money by taking advantage of Nevada's lack of state income tax. Because I spent more than fifty percent of my time in Nevada, if I were to purchase a small condo instead of continuing to rent, I could establish state residency in Nevada, which would save us several thousand dollars of Arizona state income tax per year. The condo would also be a good investment. Others in the trust company who were also doing the two-city shuffle with their out-of-state spouses had done the same, and my CPA confirmed that this was not only legitimate but advisable.

Given my CPA's recommendation, I proposed this idea to my wife. Once again, the conversation was a disaster. It didn't matter how many thousands of dollars were at stake, my proposal came across not only as me doing an end-run around my wife, but also as me taking a further step to separate myself from my wife. (My accepting the job in Nevada had apparently been the first step, regardless of the fact that we had both agreed at the time.) Nothing that I could say was going to change that perception. I had totally blown that communication. What little trust that hadn't already eroded away was now gone, and it wasn't coming back.

From this point on, my wife and I both mentally checked out. We continued to go through the motions of staying married, but we were basically living as roommates. I went ahead with the Nevada residency, because it made sense financially and because there was no trust left to save in my marriage. I bought a brand new condo and some used furniture, and I moved my work clothes and my second set of toiletries from the rented apartment over to the condo. I updated my car registration and my voter registration and joined a local gym, and with that, my income was no longer subject to Arizona state income tax.

And then COVID hit. COVID-19 had been making headlines in the news, but by early 2020, seemingly overnight, it had gone from a flu-like virus contained within China to a highly contagious global pandemic that was killing hundreds of thousands of people, and that number was rising fast. One afternoon, Braden sent an email to everyone in the trust company instructing us that we should all pack up everything and go home. We should take with us whatever we needed to be able to work from home for the foreseeable future. Nobody knew when we would be coming back to the office, but it could be weeks, maybe more. We should take our potted plants.

My office and my brand new condo were located in the Las Vegas metropolitan area. The entire economy in the area revolved around casinos and restaurants and entertainment and tourism. Most of the residents in the area worked in the service industry in some capacity. A shut-down of even several weeks would mean that no one would have the income or the savings or the credit score to qualify for mortgages. Housing was going to take a hit, and it could take years to bounce back. If I didn't want to lose all of the equity that I had just put into my brand new condo, I needed to act fast.

I called my Nevada real estate agent from the office, and we listed the condo immediately. Then I packed up the essentials from my office and drove to the condo. After spending a few hours on staging and doing some light cleaning, I was satisfied that the condo would show well. The next morning, I loaded up all of my work clothes and personal items into my car alongside my office essentials, I hid a condo key for my Nevada real estate agent outside the front door, and I headed south, back to Arizona.

CHAPTER NINETEEN

For Better or For Worse

Returning to Arizona removed quite a bit of stress off of my relationship with my wife. The commute stress was gone immediately. The condo sold quickly, and I changed my vehicle registration and my voter registration back to Arizona, so the residency issue was no longer a source of contention. I was also around more to help with household chores and to simply be present during weekday evenings. All of that was positive.

However, returning to Arizona introduced a whole new kind of stress into my marriage. I imagine that the experience was not unlike what military couples go through when a spouse who has been away for an extended period of time returns home. Or what older couples face when one spouse has been at home and the other spouse who has been working full-time retires. The spouse who has been at home has an established routine, and introducing the other spouse into the home full-time, even for the best of reasons, changes that dynamic.

My wife had an established routine. She had become the *de facto* head of household by virtue of her presence and my absence. My returning home disrupted all of that for her. It was disruptive for me, too. I had been functioning independently during the week and had an established routine of my own, one that was different from hers.

From the temperature of the thermostat to what time we ate dinner to who would drive when we went places together, neither of us was particularly good at subordinating our established norms to the other's. This was a recipe for a lot of tension, frustration, and argument.

I have never been in any relationship where there has been as much arguing as there was in my marriage to my wife, and it only increased now that we were in each other's company nearly all of the time. I hated the arguing. It was exhausting. More and more, I found it easier just to go along with whatever had already been established. My wife had been running the household for the past few years, and she had been doing a good job of it. None of the things that we argued about were worth the effort of fighting over. Most of the time, I found it easier not to have an opinion at all. Not to care.

One particular evening, however, on a drive home from dinner, I lost it. Typically, when my wife and I went places together, no matter which car we took, my wife preferred to drive. She had been a police patrol officer at one time, and she did not enjoy the passenger's seat. The exception was whenever we were drinking. At those times, we would choose a designated driver to remain relatively sober, and often times that would be me.

Whenever it was my turn to drive, my wife still took a fairly active role from the passenger's seat, issuing regular exclamations of "Watch out!" or "You need to change lanes!" or "Where are you going?" Some of this was justified. It was not uncommon for me to get caught up in conversation when others were in the car and to miss a turn, requiring a doubling back. Nevertheless, I found the constant stream of driving instructions wearing.

As I pulled the car into our driveway after that evening's drive home, my wife issued yet another driving instruction: "Careful!" I'm not sure what she wanted me to be careful of, I just knew that I had had enough.

"You know," I blurted, "it's a wonder that I have ever managed to drive anywhere all of these years without someone in the car to give me driving instructions!"

I don't remember exactly how the rest of that conversation went, but it wasn't pleasant, and I privately resolved to opt out of being the driver whenever possible from that moment on. However, the more I gave up in order to avoid arguing, the more my sense of who I was as an individual faded away. Just as I became a passenger in our vehicles everywhere that we went, I felt like I had handed over the keys to my sense of self and had taken my place in the passenger's seat of someone else's life. Had I not still had a strong identity at work, I felt as if I might have just disappeared altogether.

The one thing that had kept me hanging on to this marriage through all of its challenges was a resolute refusal to quit. I had already had two failed marriages. That was not a good track record. My first marriage never should have happened. It was a trauma response, and it was riddled with all kinds of wrong. But the ending of my second marriage had been my fault entirely. God had given me a gift in my second husband, and I had thrown it away. I was still not on speaking terms with God at this point in my life, yet somehow, through my past failures, I had cultivated a respect for the sanctity of marriage. As messed up as this one was, I was not going to be a runner anymore. I had sworn not only to my wife, but also to myself, that I was going to stick with my marriage, for better or for worse.

And then I failed at that.

One evening, my wife and I were watching television from our usual positions at opposite ends of the couch. We had been half watching the democratic primary presidential debate and half wasting time on our phones, me scrolling through Facebook and my wife playing games and texting with her friends. That left no more halves for interaction with each other. But after the debate ended, something in the room shifted. Some kind of door opened. The energy changed. My wife and I turned off the TV and put down our phones, and we looked at each other. Actually saw each other. And then, quite possibly for the first time, we truly communicated.

My wife's mother had passed away a few months earlier, and my wife, too, was now parentless. Having had my own recent experience of losing my mother and becoming parentless, I knew how that could stir up a lot of existential questions, and I know that it had for her. My wife had been feeling a pull to move back to her home state of Florida to be closer to her remaining family. It was a similar sentiment that had brought us to Arizona to consolidate my family after my father had died. My wife had mentioned this pull a couple of times, and she brought it up again that evening.

It was a rare, gentle, respectful conversation. A peace came over me. I asked my wife if moving back to Florida was really what she wanted to do. She said that it was. We gazed at each other with kindness and understanding. I suggested softly that she go ahead and do that. She nodded. We were quiet for a few minutes, and then, through tears, she offered, "We can still be friends, right?" I smiled through watery eyes of my own and assured her that we could.

I felt both relief and profound sadness at the same time. I felt relief that the long fight was finally over. That we could stop pretending that if we just tried hard enough or suffered long enough, our marriage would somehow make it. I felt profound sadness that another marriage was ending. That all of that hard work and trying my best and my tenacious commitment for better or for worse not to give up wasn't enough in the end. That maybe I just didn't have what it took to stick to anything. To love anyone. To love even myself.

As we navigated the challenges and emotions of separating our lives during the following weeks, my only ask of my wife was that we take our time and handle things orderly. This process would be hard enough on both of us without creating unnecessary fire drills. However, the moment that she received the green-light from her boss to relocate out of state, my wife the planner had us on the phone with our real estate agent the next day. By the end of that day, arrangements had been made to sell the house, and my soon-to-be-ex-wife-now-friend was showing me pictures of beachfront condos in Florida. What did I think of this one? How did I like that one? It was surreal, but it took my mind off of what was actually happening, and I was grateful for the distraction.

Our real estate agent, Christy, had become a dear friend of ours, having handled moves for us during our time in Arizona as well as the sale of my mother's home. Christy was sad to hear our news, but she was a pro. This was not Christy's first rodeo with divorcing couples, and she navigated the situation flawlessly. Within two weeks, we were under contract. Which meant that despite having hoped to avoid it, I now had a fire drill. I needed to find someplace to live.

I wasn't looking to buy right away. I needed to get my head sorted out before I made any kind of commitment to anything or anyone. I also wasn't in much of a space to be overly excited about real estate. I just needed a place to land. Christy was a gem. She knew of a perfect little rental property owned by one of her clients that was just coming available. It was close to where my sister lived. If I acted now, I could get into a lease ahead of the property being listed in the very competitive rental market.

Christy and I scrolled through photos of the property, and as usual, she had nailed it. The house fit my needs perfectly. It was a cute little ranch house in a decent neighborhood with a good-sized yard for the dog that I had brought into the marriage and that would be staying with me. The property had recently been renovated, and it appeared to be in excellent condition. It was set to be cleaned later that week, so Christy made arrangements for the two of us to go and see it the day after the cleaning. This was turning out to be much less of a fire drill than I had feared. If the house looked the same in person as it did in the photos, I was prepared to sign the lease that same day.

Two days before Christy and I were scheduled to look at the house, my sister called me. Judie had been incredibly supportive during the process of my marriage unraveling. She had been a compassionate listener and a safe harbor for me while successfully navigating an ongoing friendship with my wife. I was happy that Christy had found me a house near Judie's, and I was looking forward to spending more one-on-one time with my sister.

"I know you're probably not going to want to hear this," Judie said over the phone, "but I'm asking you to just give me a minute and hear me out."

Uh oh. Wherever this was headed, it didn't sound good. I really didn't have the stomach for any attempt by my sister to broker a truce in my marriage with some kind of Hail Mary reconciliation proposal. And I especially didn't want my situation with my wife to damage my relationship with my sister. Judie was the only family that I had left, and I was hanging on to that for dear life.

"Sure, what's up?" I asked, trying to sound cheerful and unalarmed. Bracing for the incoming gut punch.

"I know you're getting ready to sign a lease this week, but – you are not going to believe this – I'm looking out my window right now, and the neighbors across the street from me are moving out. They're tenants! I know the house doesn't look great from the outside, but maybe you could just come and look at it. Wouldn't it be cool to live right across the street from each other? Could you maybe just at least look?"

This was not even remotely what I had been expecting my sister to say. I was grateful for that. But Judie was right. I knew which house she was talking about, and it did look bad from the outside. Really bad. It was the eyesore of the neighborhood. The front yard was a moonscape of rocks, dirt, weeds, and a single dead tree. What window screens were present were bent and broken. The color of the house was something that I had only ever seen when changing the diapers of a newborn baby. The mismatched metal garage door had been driven-into by someone and never repaired. From behind the house, the towering rear façade of a big-box commercial building loomed over the back yard. And the neighbors who lived in the house next door played loud, heavy-metal music all the time and always seemed to have a yard full of cars and other motorized toys in various stages of disrepair. It was about the last place that I would ever consider living.

"I'll be right there," I said.

By the time that I arrived in my sister's neighborhood, the tenants were gone. Judie and I stood in her driveway, staring across the street, sizing up the empty house like the Peanuts gang sizing up Charlie Brown's Christmas tree. *It's not really all that bad, is it? Maybe if I use my imagination a little... Maybe if the owner puts in new screens... Maybe if they remove the dead tree...*

Judie was resourceful. She had already called the property management company for the HOA to try to get the owner's contact information, but they wouldn't give it to her. They did, however, promise to reach out to the owner themselves and deliver her message. I tried to sneak into the house's backyard by way of the side gate, hoping to walk around and have a look inside through the windows. But I couldn't get the gate open without making a lot of noise and attracting the attention of the neighbors with the cars and the toys and the heavy metal music and who-knows-what-else close at hand. So I hopped in my car and sped back home and set out on an online mission to track down the property owner myself.

My real estate law experience came in handy. I located the public property records easily and found the name and address of the owner. But even with my well-honed sleuthing skills, I struck out on finding a phone number or an email address. Refusing to give up that easily, I whipped up a letter to the owner expressing my interest and explaining the urgency of the timing. I jumped back in my car, and I raced to the nearest UPS store, arriving just before the cutoff for overnight delivery. I checked the box on the form for early morning, next day delivery service, and I sent my letter on its way along with a little prayer – my first prayer since I had left the ministry. And then I went home to wait.

By noon the next day, I hadn't received any response to my letter. The UPS website showed that the letter had been delivered early that morning and had been signed for by someone with an illegible signature. I re-read my letter to make sure that I hadn't made a typo in my phone number or my email address in my haste to get the letter out the door. Both looked fine. Judie called the HOA again. The HOA told her that they had left a voice mail message, but that was all that they could do.

I was scheduled to go and see the other property with Christy the next day. If I let Christy's client's property get away, I would find myself at the mercy of a very competitive rental market, and I hadn't seen much else out there that I liked. I had done everything that I could think of to reach the owner of the property across the street from my sister. There was nothing more that I could do. So, I just gave it up to God. That guy that I hadn't been speaking to. If living across the street from my sister was meant to be, I would hear from the owner. Otherwise, I would know that it wasn't meant for me, and I would go with the house that Christy had found. It was that simple.

My phone vibrated. It was my email. I had a new message from a name that I didn't recognize and had no idea how to pronounce. Spam, I assumed. But given the situation, I opened it anyway. The message wasn't from the owner of the house across the street from my sister. It was from the owner's husband, who was also the landlord. He had received my letter, and he would be happy to show me the house. I called him right away. English was clearly not a first language for him, but we did the best that we could, and we managed to make arrangements to meet at the property later that same day.

I arrived late that afternoon to find the landlord in the garage, stubbing out a cigarette and kicking a path through heaps of junk. He beamed with pride and was excited to walk me through the house. I had invited Judie to join us, and the landlord guided us from room to room, gesturing theatrically as he drew our attention to various features and amenities.

The inside wasn't as bad as the front yard or the garage had been. It was worse. Ten times worse! There was junk piled everywhere. Every surface was filthy. The walls were full of holes. The window blinds were trashed. The HVAC vents were caked with lint and dust. I could hardly breathe through the smell of cigarette smoke that permeated every room. How on earth had anyone lived in this? How could I?

But the electricity was working. The plumbing was working. The air conditioning was working. The roof didn't appear to leak. And when I stood in the living room and looked out through the foggy front window, I was looking directly into the front window of my sister's house.

"I'll take it!" I said. With a few conditions, of course.

CHAPTER TWENTY

Pride

I moved into the house across the street from my sister on Halloween of 2020, and I spent my first evening sitting in the driveway with my dog, handing out candy to passing trick-or-treaters, while my sister did the same from her own driveway. Dozens of families paraded through with their little monsters and princesses and movie characters and with dogs of their own, and they introduced themselves to me. Everyone knew Judie, who had lived in her house for over twenty years, and they all were happy to have another Simpson in the neighborhood. I could not have asked for a warmer welcome.

My wife had left for Florida the week before I had moved out of our marital home and into this one, and that last week had been rough. As I watched my soon-to-be-ex-wife and her moving truck drive away forever, I could not have felt more alone in that empty house. The world was still in the throes of COVID. My work was conducted entirely via video conference, and in-person social interactions were frowned upon. Families and friends were polarized over their choices of fearful isolation or suspicious defiance. All of humanity was feeling disquiet and out of sorts. The social climate of COVID had only deepened my own feelings of disorientation, loss, failure, and brokenness.

Living across the street from my sister was cathartic, providing me with just the right balance of the company of family and the independence that I needed to rebuild a life of my own. Living steps from each other's front doors also made it easy for Judie and me to get together for dinner and wine, and we did that at least twice a week. Those evenings became special times for the two of us to bond as sisters. Judie and I had not been close as teenagers or as young adults, and the closeness that we had developed in more recent years had revolved around caring for Mom and Dad and handling myriad estate matters after our parents had passed. The time that we had now was our time, as adult siblings, and we each discovered in the other someone with whom we could admit our imperfections and lean on our shared experiences to help each other work through past struggles and present challenges and opportunities.

Judie was a strong Christian, and she expressed her faith with love and compassion, with no hint of the judgment that I had felt from my parents. She provided me with a safe space to have open conversations about identity and sexuality and spirituality without condemnation. With Judie, I had an environment in which I could engage in self-examination without feeling any pressure to hurry up and have it all figured out right away. This was refreshing, and it tilled the ground for my healing.

The living environment in my house, however, was another matter. Even after having the place professionally deep-cleaned, it still felt dirty, and the stifling smell of cigarette smoke was inescapable. Windows wouldn't open. Power outlets didn't work. The oven was installed incorrectly and was unusable. The washing machine didn't get clothes clean. The cabinetry was falling apart. Dust and debris spewed from the vents. The yard looked like death. And the landlord did not see problems in any of this. When a kitchen drawer fell apart in my hands for the third time on Thanksgiving Day, I came apart right along with it. I could not live like this sustainably. It was unhealthy physically, and it was unhealthy mentally. I saw only two options: I could buy the house, tear it and the yard down to studs and dirt, and redo everything, or I could find someplace else to live.

As daunting as option one sounded, option two was untenable. Living across the street from my sister was a balm for my soul like no other that I had found, and I couldn't emotionally afford to give that up. At least not now, not at this time in my life when I was so vulnerable and fragile that I feared I might crumble up and blow away but for the lifeline of proximity to my sister. My survival depended upon the viability of option one. I would have to be strategic in how I went about this. And I could use a little help from God. That guy that I was still barely speaking to, but who had helped me to get into this house in the first place. Maybe He could help me again.

The first thing that I did was to write another letter to my landlord and his wife. Given the language barrier, I figured a letter would give them the opportunity to fully digest my words and to understand clearly what I had in mind. I wrote to them about how happy I was to be living in this house, how grateful to them I was for this opportunity, and how much it meant to me to live across the street from my sister, especially now that our parents had passed and we each were all of the family that the other had. I asked them if they would consider entertaining an offer to sell the house to me. I suggested that we could do the deal ourselves, which made my offer six percent more attractive to them than if they were to sell the home the traditional way. I sent my letter off via email, along with another little prayer, and I was elated when my landlord responded a few days later that they were indeed open to considering an offer.

Now, it was real strategy time. The stakes were high, but only for me, which is not a strong place from which to negotiate. I figured that in this situation, simplicity was my friend. The fewer points of negotiation involved, the more likely it was that I could shepherd a deal through without my landlord or his wife getting cold feet. I started with a call to Christy, and she was kind enough to help me with valuation. I then ordered a home inspection, both to ensure that there were no hidden issues and to support my offering price with an impartial report of the home's true condition. Finally, I got myself fully preapproved for a loan. I packaged all of this up, and I sent it off to my landlord and his wife along with a clean offer – no contingencies, no repairs requested – and another little prayer. The only term that we had to negotiate was price. After some back and forth, my landlord, his wife, and I all agreed on a price that was a little higher than I had hoped, but that was within the range that Christy had thought was reasonable. We would close right after the first of the year.

I was so excited! All that was left to do was to think of the perfect way to share the news with my sister. As much as Judie and I had talked about so many important things, I had managed to keep my efforts to purchase the home a secret, hoping to be able to surprise her with good news. Christmas was just over a week away now, and it presented the perfect opportunity. Judie and I would be spending that Christmas together, just the two of us.

I remembered a keychain that I had received from my title company, one of those promotional items that businesses give away. That would be perfect! I placed it into a small box, and I wrapped it up in decorative paper. On Christmas day, I hid my little box deep the Christmas tree, the last gift to be opened. I watched expectantly with barely contained enthusiasm as my sister unwrapped the box, lifted the lid, and removed the metal keychain that was engraved with the logo of my title company.

"What is this?" She looked puzzled.

"It's a keychain!" I stated the obvious.

"Oh…" Judie struggled to express confused appreciation for my gift. "Uhm… why are you giving me a keychain?"

"Why would I give you a keychain from a title company?" I challenged my sister to think. I knew that Judie was extremely smart. I knew that she wouldn't need any more than that to get it.

"Hmmm… why would you give me a keychain from a title company…?" she repeated, mostly to herself.

I watched the wheels turning in her mind. And then I saw the lightbulb come on.

"You bought the house? You bought the house?! Oh my God, you bought the house!"

My sister leapt to her feet and threw her arms around me. We hugged and cried all over each other. She didn't give the keychain back to me. She wasn't mad that I hadn't involved her. Judie's response was one hundred percent pure joy. This was the best Christmas ever!

The moment that I closed on the house, the remodel began. I did a lot of the demolition myself, but I left the building to the professionals. I lived in that house along with my dog and two cats throughout the entire remodel, at one point having one working toilet, a refrigerator, and a microwave, but no other working plumbing or appliances in the house. I set up a card table and a bucket and a hose in the backyard for washing up, and I showered at my sister's house. For most people, this would have been a nightmarish living situation. I, however, was in heaven. The sounds of saws and hammers, the smell of sawdust, and the constant state of construction projects in progress brought me right back to happy times at Lake Pillsbury. I migrated my work set-up around the house from room to room in order to keep the noise and mess from being a distraction on my video calls. When things got really loud, I would take my laptop and my animals across the street and work from my sister's house. I had a lot of fun with that remodel. I got to exercise the creative side of my brain, and I got to remake the house exactly as I liked without having to justify any of it to anyone.

On one particularly ordinary morning, I was going about my work-day from a quiet corner of the house when an email message arrived in my inbox from an outside sender. The message was from a recruiter, and she was representing a company that was looking for someone to serve as its president. Did I know anyone who might be interested? I closed the email. I was very happy in my current role. Working with

Braden was a dream experience, and I could have been happy working with him for the rest of my career.

However, I didn't delete the email. It continued to sit in my inbox and in my mind for the next week. Braden was young, extremely talented, and highly respected within the company. It was only a matter of time before he would be promoted. When that happened, one of two things would follow: either I would be promoted into his role, or someone else would take the role. If someone else took the role, I may or may not be happy working under that person. If I were promoted into the role, there was a good chance that I would be leading that trust company without Braden's direct involvement. Either way, my days of working closely with Braden were likely numbered. If I pursued the recruiter's opportunity, I might have more control over the outcome for me. I at least owed it to myself to inquire.

I made the call. The opportunity was more attractive than I thought, in terms of both compensation and where that company was headed. The parent company was in a rapid growth phase, with merger and acquisition activity underway that would soon catapult the company onto a national stage. The parent company needed someone who could lead the company into that promised land, and they were very interested in me. I had the résumé they were looking for, and I had the leadership experience and the entrepreneurial boldness to do the job. After a many-months-long interview process, I accepted their offer.

I could hardly believe it. I was going to be president of a company, and I would be leading it into important industry territory in the near future. The vow that I had made to myself to build a professional legacy that my parents would be proud of was coming to fruition. I was going to be somebody. Not quite at the same level as my sister, but much closer. Judie was thrilled for me, and she was very proud of me. If I couldn't hear those words from my mother, it felt really good to hear them from my sister. Maybe now I was finally on track to do something worthy of that pride.

It broke my heart to share my news with Braden. He had been so very good to me, and he had been grooming me as a potential candidate to succeed him when the time came. It broke my heart even more to take two of my colleagues with me, leaving a big hole in Braden's leadership team. But I had a leadership team of my own to build now, and I needed those two leaders in order to take the company where I had committed to take it within the time frame prescribed. To Braden's credit, he was very gracious, giving me sound advice and connecting me with industry contacts who could help me to succeed.

Leading a company at this level brought a whole new level of stress right along with it. Unlike the public company that I had just come from, this company's parent company was largely owned by a team of private equity investors who took a great deal of interest in the day-to-day goings on of the organization. This company in particular was under scrutiny both from our regulators and from our M&A due diligence folks. There was very little room to screw up. As stressful as that environment was, it was also confidence-building. I had built a strong and tight senior leadership team, and I had reorganized the company to capitalize on everyone's strengths and to bolster employee engagement. I knew that this team was fully capable of executing on what we needed to do to reach our most important goal on time. And when we did reach that goal, with only days to spare, it felt good to have proven to myself, and subconsciously to my now-deceased parents, that I was capable of leading at that level.

There is a popular saying that pride comes before a fall. This phrase is actually adapted from a longer Biblical passage, but the implication is the same, and shortly after achieving the company's most important near-term goal, the phrase applied to me. With both business success and industry recognition, I had gotten a little bit too comfortable in my position, while at the same time feeling uncomfortable with my peers in the parent company. As much as I longed to belong, I just didn't feel like I fit in with that crowd. To compensate, I drank more than I should have at a private social event where my peers were present, and I let my guard down. The next thing I knew, somebody thought I said something that I didn't, and my credibility with my colleagues was compromised. That meant that my effectiveness as a leader would be compromised also. The damage was done. There was no scenario in which this would end well. I did what needed to be done for the good of everyone concerned, and I resigned.

CHAPTER TWENTY-ONE

Into the Water

When I resigned from my role as company president, I felt the hopeless shame of failure like I never had before. There was no one at whose feet I could lay any part of the blame for my downfall other than myself. Even God wasn't getting the blame for this one. I had let the best professional opportunity of my life slip through my hands because I had asked more of professional success than it had to give. I had expected my accomplishments to create an identity for me, and when I had found no identity there, in even my highest accomplishment, I had stumbled, and I had fallen, all the way down to my own personal rock bottom.

I sat alone in my family room, silent and still. Not trying to solve anything or even to process anything. Just letting the emotions and the thoughts come on their own. I was devastated. The inventory of my self-worth was completely decimated. I had no career. No proud parents. No spouse. No music. And no God. I realized for the first time how badly the life that I had been trying to build for myself was taking on water.

From my earliest memories of trying to be a little adult to the pride that had come from "making it" in the professional world, I had tethered my identity to my own abilities and accomplishments. When I had excelled in something, whether it was a talent or a profession or a personal relationship, I had had a sense of being somebody. When

I had failed, I had raced as fast as I could to excel in something else. A new credential. A new skill. A new career. A new relationship. In between successes, I had done everything in my power to create at least the appearance of holding everything all together, hoping that maybe no one would notice that I had temporarily ceased to exist.

All of this activity had been happening on the surface. Whenever a storm came, I had simply raced away from it, searching for smoother waters, never stopping to address the damage that the storm had inflicted, not only on me but on those around me. Now, my boat was sinking. I could not ignore the damage any longer. There were simply too many holes. There was only one thing left to do. I had to jump overboard. Abandon the boat that I had been building my whole life. Untether myself from the badly listing vessel of my self-manufactured identity and just jump into the water. If I didn't, my sinking boat would take me down with it.

I cut the tether, and I jumped. No racing to the next career. No racing to the next relationship. I had to dive straight down into the water and explore the depths of my soul. I had to understand what I was truly seeking before I could have any hope of leaving behind all of the behaviors that had kept me racing around aimlessly on the surface of the water, leaving a wake of destruction behind me. As my feet left the boat and my hands broke the surface of the water, I cried out to God. I didn't know what to ask for, so I just asked Him to show me what I needed to see. And then I plunged beneath the surface and swam down into the depths.

I would love to say that with that jump, everything became clear, instantly and all at once. It didn't. The waters of my soul were no bright blue, shallow, Caribbean waters. These were the cold, murky waters of the deep. To truly get my bearings, I was going to be down here for a while. I was grateful for two things that God had already provided for me. The first was my wonderful sister, who was there to listen and to support me and to love me through this life-changing part of my journey. The second was the financial means to be able to take a break from gainful employment so that I could devote my full attention to finding my way through the murk.

Below the surface now, my light was on, ready to explore, but I didn't know where to begin. I tried to take stock of my surroundings, but there was so much clouding the water that I couldn't make out anything. To clear out a layer of murk, I decided to start with something tangible, something that I could see: I started with a physical purge. I thought about all of the boxes and stacks of items that had been in Tevye's home, and how heavily that excess physical ballast had weighed him down mentally and emotionally. I could not afford any excess ballast. I went through every box and every single item in my house and in my garage, and I threw away most of it. I went way beyond Marie Kondo and even got rid of most things that sparked joy. Out of a dozen boxes of photos and letters and greeting cards, I kept a single manilla envelope of the most treasured mementos. Every journal and tablet and scrap of paper containing everything that I had ever written went into the trash. Every article of clothing that I hadn't worn in the past year, and even some that I had, went to Goodwill. Eighty percent of my books found new homes, and I probably held onto too many of those. If an item wasn't a home furnishing, a tool, a kitchen essential, a wardrobe essential, or something that I used regularly, it was gone.

The one exception to this purge was backpacking items. I had always loved to spend time in the outdoors – the more remote and less populated, the better. The wilderness was right up there with Lake Pillsbury as a place where I could go to do my best thinking, and I also had many fond memories of backpacking with my dad. Seeing those backpacking items laid out in the "keep" pile gave me an idea: that summer would be a good time for me to take a backpacking trip. Perhaps some time in the wilderness was exactly what I needed to facilitate a deeper dive into my mental and emotional murk.

My backpacking trips in the past had all been either with Dad or with our family friend Larry, and sometimes with both of them. On all of those trips, there had been established roles. The men would plan the trip, decide where we would go on which days, decide what we would eat, decide who would carry which community items, navigate the hikes, set up camp, gather wood, make fires, and cook the meals. I was always the only woman. My role was to pack and carry my own belongings, set up my own sleeping tent, clean up after our meals, and otherwise follow dutifully along behind the men. I had enjoyed those trips immensely, but because so many key responsibilities had been handled by the men, there were big gaps in my knowledge and experience. If backpacking were to continue to be something that I enjoyed, I needed to fill in those gaps.

To solve this, I enrolled in an online course that taught backpacking fundamentals. While a lot of the learning material was familiar to me, the course accomplished the much-needed job of filling in the holes of my backpacking knowledge. Best of all, the course culminated in a five-day wilderness trip through the eastern Sierra-Nevada mountain range with a small group of several of my classmates from around the country.

During the weeks leading up to the trip, I continued to sluice through the murky waters in my home and in my head while also managing my ongoing home remodel, but I also enjoyed having something lighter to look forward to. I collected, sorted, and weighed all of the items for my trip, and I practiced my newly-acquired wayfinding skills on my local hiking trails.

For purposes of dividing course participants into hiking groups, the organizers matched students according to their backpacking abilities, with the idea that it would be most enjoyable for people to hike with others who kept a roughly similar pace. To best accomplish this sorting of students into compatible hiking groups, the organizers asked us pointed questions about our past backpacking trips. I had done most of my backpacking at a much younger age, and most of the information about the distance, speed, and elevation gain that comprised an average day for me was lost with the passing of my father. I looked back over topographical maps of the areas where Dad and I had hiked, trying to recall the routes and attempting to piece together the requested information. I also asked Larry to help me with data from more recent trips that he and I had taken together. I provided all of this to the trip organizers along with the caveat that these were estimates. It was the best that I could do.

When the day of the trip arrived, I was ready. I had ramped up my CrossFit workouts and had been running several miles nearly every day. I had purchased lighter and more modern backpacking gear, and I had practiced setting up and taking down my new, ultralight tent. After a guide had inspected everyone's setup to make sure that nothing was missing and that nobody's rig was grossly overweight, our group of ten hikers and two guides set off down the trail.

The first day went great! After a full day of hiking with multiple stops for snacks, water, and practical backpacking lessons, I was dog tired, but not sore, and I was enjoying many interesting conversations with my new friends. The second day was another story. I started having trouble hiking uphill early in the day, and by the afternoon, I struggled to keep up with my group. The third day was worse. Downhill hiking was fine, but uphill hiking was making me nauseous. So much so that one of the guides broke off and hiked with me while the rest of the group went ahead.

At first, my guides suspected that I might be experiencing altitude sickness. But after running through a list of typical symptoms, mine didn't add up. Besides that, I had hiked at that altitude all of my life, and I had never experienced even a hint of altitude sickness. One of the guides wondered about possible anemia. However, because altitude sickness had been such a hot topic in the online class, I had begun taking iron supplements ahead of the trip to facilitate altitude adaptation. With the extra iron that I had been taking, anemia was unlikely. One of our guides had also had COVID recently, and we wondered if that might be a possibility. But I had no cough, no shortness of breath, and no other COVID-like symptoms, so that theory didn't make sense either. We collectively concluded that some combination of altitude

sickness and/or anemia was the likely culprit, and that I would probably feel better in the next couple of days with lower altitude hiking
coming up.

I put on a brave smile and kept going as well as I could, but I was
disheartened. I had come into this trip so full of hope for a healing
experience, but instead, my feelings of inadequacy began to creep back
in. Had I overestimated the difficulty of my past hikes? Had I overestimated my abilities at my current age compared to younger years?
Was something else going on? Whatever it was, I felt like I was that
weak, small, sickly kid who nobody really wanted on their team, all
over again. I couldn't even do something healing and light and maybe
even a little fun without screwing it up. My fellow hikers were gracious
and kind, and my guides were very supportive – and were also glad that
I hung in there and finished the hike each day so that neither of them
had to leave the group to extract me from the trip. Still, I felt like an
anchor that was holding my group back from hiking as far and as fast
as some of them wanted to go. Like they all would have been better off
if I weren't there.

By the fourth day, my symptoms were worse, and I began to get
the sense that I was in real trouble. I had completely lost my appetite.
Without calories, how would I have the strength to hike at all? As our
group was getting ready to set out for the day, I threw up, and my iron
supplement came up with it. This was not surprising, because I had
taken the supplement on an empty stomach. But in that moment, a
still, small voice stirred inside my mind. Outside of multivitamins, I
had never taken iron supplements before, but I was taking the maximum recommended dose for high-altitude hiking as a preventative
measure in response to all of the talk in the course about altitude
sickness. If I were indeed experiencing some combination of altitude
sickness and/or anemia, it seemed important that I find a way to keep
that iron supplement down. But what if the opposite were true? What
if I were taking in more iron than my body could handle? Should I try
to choke down another supplement on the altitude sickness/anemia

theory, or could I actually be overdosing myself? The group was ready to leave. I needed to make a decision.

I remembered what I had asked God when I dove into the water. "Show me what I need to see." I had no background in medicine, nutrition, biology, or chemistry. I was taking an over-the-counter supplement, and I was within the recommended dosage that was printed on the box. I knew from the backpacking class that nausea and vomiting were symptoms of altitude sickness, and one of my guides had shared that those were symptoms of anemia as well. Everything was pointing to altitude sickness and/or anemia. So why had iron poisoning, something that I knew nothing about, come into my mind in that moment? Was it possible that God was showing me something that I needed to see?

I decided to listen to that still, small voice, and I didn't take any more supplements. Within twenty-four hours, the nausea went away, and my appetite returned nearly as quickly. By the last day of the trip, I had regained nearly all of my strength, and I was able to keep up with the group. By the time that I returned home to Arizona, too many days had passed since I had taken my last supplement to test whether the culprit had been iron poisoning. However, from what I've learned since then, if iron poisoning was indeed the culprit – and I am now convinced that it was – and if I had continued to take those high-dose supplements while taxing my body at that level of activity, I may not have made it out of that trip alive.

In so many ways, that backpacking trip was a sad disappointment. I had really been looking forward to being out in the wilderness, getting some great physical exercise, meeting new friends, and having lots of time to think. Instead, I had spent the trip feeling nauseous and inadequate, trailing too far behind the group to develop meaningful friendships, and having no ability to think about anything other than making it through each day.

However, even with all of that, one profoundly important thing did come out of that trip, and it was worth the price of all of the struggle. Since the day that I left the ministry in 1996, I had spent nearly thirty years blindly navigating life on my own, not speaking to God. A few months prior to that backpacking trip, I had ventured a few tiny, hesitant prayers in the process of renting and then buying the house across the street from my sister. Then, after I resigned as company president, when I could no longer deny that my boat was sinking, I had thrown open the door to my connection with God as I dove into the water. After all of those years, I had finally started speaking to God again. But on that backpacking trip, when listening to that still, small voice likely saved my life, I realized that I was not the only one who was doing the talking.

CHAPTER TWENTY-TWO

The Waters of
the Deep

After I returned from my backpacking trip, with the physical purge of my home – and now also of my body – completed, it was time to dive deeper, to venture into mental and emotional waters. But now I had an unexpected form of help. I had a newfound dialogue with God. I had no idea how to talk with God. The Lord's Prayer seemed too formal, and it certainly wasn't a dialogue. I wasn't sure that the way that I had prayed in the spirit back in my ministry days was even real. I finally settled on just having an ordinary conversation with God. Since I wasn't the only one doing the talking, I decided that it was time for me to bombard God with questions of the non-rhetorical variety. Why had I failed at everything that I had tried? Why was I stuck in a seemingly endless feedback loop of insanity, doing the same thing over and over again and expecting a different result? Why had so many things started out bright and then faded to the blackest form of darkness? Why could I never manage to be more than a bright little flash in the pan? Was there some big, overarching answer that I had been completely missing? I sat down in the family room of my now-uncluttered home, looking out the back window of my now-green back yard. "God, show me what I need to see."

As with my approach to the physical purge of my home, I began with the things that were easiest for me to see. I ticked through the chronology of my various careers, looking for themes, starting with music, my earliest and purest career love. There was nothing about my dance with music that had felt wrong. It had never even felt like work – it was that sweet. So why had music had such power to bring me to my knees? Did music have too much power over me still? Was it too emotionally dangerous for me to ever be able to interact with music again? Oh, this question was much more charged than I thought it would be. Maybe I should have started with an easier one.

God answered. "My child, I gave you your love for music. It is a gift that I designed uniquely for you, and I gave it to you on the day that you were born. I want you to have it. I want you to love it. I want it to be your favorite special gift from Me. But take care that you do not make music your god. 'I am the Lord, your God. You shall have no other gods before Me.' I gave you this commandment to keep you safe. To make sure that you would never have to be at the mercy of another god who would hurt you or let you down. Go, love your music. Just keep it in its place."

"Well, what about my time with the ministry, God? I gave up my career in music for You! I was going to live my whole life for You. I followed every instruction. I did everything that I was asked to do. And then it turned to hell. Where were You then?"

God answered. "You did well to obey your leaders and to submit to them. You also did well to discern works of evil. Those works are Mine to deal with, and those leaders will have to give an account. Being vigilant is important if you are going to fulfill your ministry, but so is endurance. You have to stay in the race in order to finish it and to claim your reward. I will never leave you or forsake you, but whenever you leave and you take your light with you, I can't use it in that situation."

"So, what am I supposed to do now? I have no career, not even a job. I have all of these credentials and all of these skills, but I'm not even sure that I like any of the careers that go with them. How did I end up here, and what should I do now?"

God answered. "Take care not to think too highly of your own abilities; that is when you stumble. All of your professional endeavors have been an attempt to prove yourself worthy in the eyes of others. In order to be great among others, you must humble yourself and steward the gifts that I have given you with the heart of a servant. Others may approve of you, or they may exclude you, but remember that not all praise by others is good. The approval that matters is Mine. My approval is not something that you can earn; I have already given it to you by My grace. Throw off your shame and present yourself upright as a worker whom I have approved."

God sure had a lot to say about career-related things. I was extremely grateful to hear that I could keep my relationship with music after all, albeit in its proper place. I also got the sense that work and ministry are actually two sides of the same coin: servitude. I needed to turn my lens around from focusing on myself and my own abilities and shortcomings to focusing on using my gifts to serve others.

It was time now to see what God had to say about a murkier topic: relationships. Why had I had such a hard time connecting with people? Why couldn't I forge a deeper relationship with my parents? Why had I continued to strike out in love? What about this whole sexuality thing? Why didn't I ever feel like I belonged anywhere? And why did all of that matter so much? Should it?

God answered. "My daughter, I love you. I knew you even before I formed you. I know every hair on your head; I put every one of them in place Myself. You are My handiwork. My masterpiece. You are beautiful and precious to Me, and I am so proud of you.

"Hear this, My daughter: I created you for love. My love for you is a perfect love, and it is the only perfect love. It is unconditional – you cannot earn it, neither can you lose it. Your quest for love has never been about sexuality; you have been seeking the kind of intimate love from people that only I can give, and you have searched for it everywhere in vain.

"You already have My everlasting love in infinite measure. If you want to experience the depth of My love, you must give love. Extend to others the grace that I have given to you. Manifest My love freely and generously, without fear, and allow others to reflect My love back to you and to help you in your times of need. Only then will you truly experience the intimate, perfect love that you are seeking."

God was giving me a lot to think about. I guess I had been expecting my parents to be God, to be perfect, and to love me perfectly. Maybe I hadn't actually wanted to know them, because that would have meant finding out that they weren't perfect. Maybe I had been so focused on receiving love from my parents that I had never given them the grace to allow them or even to want them to be human. For that matter, maybe I had been so focused on proving myself worthy to receive love from everyone around me that I had never learned how to give love at all. No wonder my close relationships hadn't worked. No wonder I hadn't found intimacy in sexuality. No wonder I hadn't felt like I belonged anywhere. The theme was becoming even more clear: I needed to turn my lens around from focusing on my own yearning to receive love to focusing on giving love.

Now it was time for me to ask God the really hard questions.

"God, You've been talking a lot about how I should relate with others and with the world around me. But what about You? How do I relate to You? Who are You, anyway? And while we're at it, who am I?"

God answered. "Ah, My child, I've been waiting for you to ask Me this question. You have been on a journey to find your identity. You want to know who you are. Who do you think that you are?"

"I don't know! That was a dumb question, God. If I knew, why would I be on a journey to find out? And why would I be asking You?"

"How will you know?"

"How will I know who I am? I don't know that either, God. I thought I was a musician, but that fell apart. Then I thought I was going to be a minister for You, but we both know how that turned out. Then I thought I was a lawyer and a business person, but none of those occupations really defined me. I was my parents' daughter, but they're dead. At least I'm still a sister, thank God... ehr... I mean, thank You. I was a wife, but I've been divorced three times now. Heck, no one could even figure out whether I was gay or not, including me half of the time. So, I don't know how I'll know."

"Do you want to be defined by those things?"

"By profession? By relationship? By sexuality? No, absolutely not! I don't want to be defined by a skill or a role or a desire or a behavior. I don't want to be stuffed into someone else's tidy little box and labeled and filed neatly into a category of characteristics. I'm so much more than that!"

"So, how do you want to be defined?"

"I don't know... I just am! I don't want to be a nobody, I want to be *somebody*, but not somebody who people limit with a definition. I just want to stand up and say, 'I exist, I am!'"

"Now you are getting somewhere."

"What? God, You are not making any sense. I don't even understand You. Who are You, anyway?"

"I am."

"You are... what?"

"I am."

"What do You mean, 'I am?' God, that is the stupidest answer that You've given me all day. How am I supposed to know who You are if all You say is, 'I am?'"

"Isn't that what you said that you want for yourself?"

"Well, yes, but..."

"I am. And because I am in you, therefore, you are."

"Okay... wait... hold on... Can we go back to You for a minute? So, who You are is not defined or limited by anything outside of Yourself? Is that what You're saying?"

"Yes."

"So... then... because You are, and because You are in me, that's why I'm having such a hard time finding an identity for myself that the world understands?"

"What do you think?"

"Oh my God, God, You are so frustrating! I am the one asking the questions here. Why can't You just give me a direct answer for once?"

"What do you think?"

"Aaaaagh! You are a broken frickin' record, God! I have had it with this conversation! I guess I'm just going to have to figure this one out for myself."

———————

While I was having my conversations with God, I also continued to manage my ongoing home remodel, and I had begun to look for employment as well. I wasn't necessarily seeking a career-defining role, but given the torn-up state of my home, an infusion of capital would be needed in the near future if I didn't want to continue house-camping indefinitely.

I reached out to a few of the connections in my professional network, and before I knew it, I was on the phone with the president of another trust company. They were looking to hire a leader, and the president and I initially chatted about that open role, but she had another idea. The trust company's parent company was exploring a type of estate planning product that it was considering introducing company-wide, and my knowledge and experience were the perfect fit to develop that product and lead the rollout. Would I be interested?

This sounded like a project that I would enjoy immensely, and more importantly, the proposed product would be of great service to the company's clients. My background in business, law, and product development made me uniquely suited for the role. Yes, I would definitely be interested. After months of conversations up and down the ladder of leaders associated with this project, the company created the role, and I was hired into it.

I enjoyed my new role. I loved the leader that I worked with, the culture was one where both clients and employee well-being were prioritized, and I had an opportunity to add real value both to the company and to clients' lives. I enjoyed the work even more because I wasn't tying my identity to my role. This role was a way for me to serve, and I could do it well.

It took less than a month for the first test to be thrown at me. The company was in the midst of restructuring the way that it evaluated and managed business objectives, and the project that I had been hired to lead was defunded just three weeks after I started. I had a few additional weeks to shrink-wrap and shelve all of the research that had been done on the project, and then my role would be defunded as well. In the past, the collateral damage to my sense of self-worth would have been devastating. Now that I had decoupled my identity from my career, there was still damage, but at nowhere near the level that it would have been. My primary concern now was simply retaining gainful employment.

Happily for me, the company valued the talent that I brought to the table, and my leaders didn't want to lose me any more than I wanted to lose my job. We found another initiative within the company that needed leadership at my level, and while I wasn't a great fit for that role, I could do the job. We made the transfer, and I assumed my role with the new initiative under a different leader.

A few months after my work situation settled down, the next test came. Through all of my career turmoil, and through all of my conversations with God thus far, my sister had been a rock-solid source of support. During our many evenings sharing dinner together, Judie had encouraged me and cheered for me and listened with an open mind and an open heart while I talked through everything that was happening. Our relationship as sisters had blossomed into a deep friendship, and I was enjoying Judie's company immensely. I was equally happy to be there for her also as she talked through the triumphs and trials of her own life.

On one such evening, Judie had returned that afternoon from a business trip to Texas, and I had walked across the street to her house to join her for dinner. I had recently signed off on the last punch list item for my remodel, and now that my house was finally just the way I wanted it, Judie and I had been enjoying alternating evenings between our two homes. Tonight, it was Judie's turn to host.

"I have some news to share with you," Judie said as we were finishing up dinner.

"I'm all ears!"

"I'm just going to come right out and tell you, and then we can talk about it." Judie paused. Then she announced, "I'm moving to Texas."

I was stunned. My sister had lived in the house where we were now sitting for the past twenty-something years. After my parents had died, Judie's house had become "the family home" for me by default. In all of my moves and through all of my life changes, Judie's home had always been stable. Even Judie had been certain that she would live in that house for the rest of her life. And now that would be changing.

I remembered my conversations with God. Instead of immediately turning my mental lens to how this would impact me, I stayed focused on Judie as she went on to tell me about the business opportunities that were opening up to her. She was entering into a new phase of her career, and Texas made perfect sense for her. Judie's own sense of identity was also evolving, and leaving some of her old baggage behind in Arizona would give her a healthy springboard from which to continue to grow. These sounded like all of the right reasons and none of the wrong ones.

I told Judie that I was truly happy for her, and I meant it. We hugged and we cried, and we spent the rest of the evening talking about other things. There would be plenty of time to process logistics and emotions later. We just wanted to spend the rest of that evening like any other, hanging out together and being sisters.

When I left Judie's house that evening to walk across the street to my own, I turned around to take a look at what would soon no longer be my family home. My sister was standing in the doorway, waving good night to me, just like Mom and Dad had always done. I waved back to her. Then I turned and walked the rest of the way across the street and in through the front door of my freshly remodeled home, and I bawled.

CHAPTER TWENTY-THREE

The House on the Ditch

"God, what are You doing?!" I screamed as I flopped down in a family room chair. "My sister was the only thing that I had left in the whole world, and now You're taking her away from me too!" I was so angry with God. "I have nothing here. Nothing! I barely got a leg up again in a role where I could shine, and You cut that right out from under me in three weeks. Three weeks, God! But even that wasn't enough for You. Oh no, You had to go and take my sister away from me too. I have nothing left now, God. Nothing but You!"

I was furious with God. I really was happy for my sister, but I felt like all of the work that I had been doing to find myself over these past few months had been reduced to naught. It had all been nothing more than an enormous waste of time. Why had I even bothered to talk with God in the first place if all He was going to do was tease me with a fresh start, only to jerk it away again, and then take away the only family that I had left.

"What is wrong with You?!" I railed. "What kind of a God does this to people? What am I supposed to do now?"

God answered. "Was that question rhetorical?"

"Oh, now You pipe up! Why are You speaking to me, God? Go away!"

God challenged. "Choose your God."

"What? What are you even saying?!"

"Choose your God."

"Oh, and I suppose You want me to choose You. You! The One who took away everything and everyone that I ever loved and cared about! And now you want me to choose You? Ha! What are you smoking, God?"

"Who else would you choose? Yourself? How has that been working out?"

"Well, if You would just get out of the way and stop taking everything away from me, then I could…"

"You could what?"

"I could… I don't know, maybe make something of myself for once!"

"What would you make?"

"I don't know! Why are you asking me all of these questions?"

I cried and cried. Now not only did I have nothing left but God, but I was back in one of these confusing conversations with Him where all He did was ask me questions and make cryptic statements like "I am," and "Choose your God." I cried until I had no more tears left, and then I just sat in the dark, in silence.

God spoke. "Arise, My child, and walk with Me. I have something to show you."

What did I have to lose? There was truly nothing left to lose at this point. I stood up, and I walked out my front door. I walked down the street, and I walked along the winding path in my neighborhood park. The park was one of the only sources of anything green or alive or inviting in a neighborhood lined with endless rows of brown houses, brown rocks, prickly cacti, and patches of fake grass. There were pine trees in the park. I hadn't really paid them much attention before. As I walked along, I wondered how it was that pine trees managed to grow in this part of Arizona, where temperatures would climb into the one-hundred-and-teens for weeks on end. These must be some different kind of pine trees than the ones around Lake Pillsbury or in the little mountain town of Twain Harte where I had lived near my parents. I had really liked Twain Harte. I sure wasn't going to stay in this Arizona furnace by myself. If I were going to be totally alone, I could at least be alone someplace that I liked. I made a mental note to look into Twain Harte after my walk. After God had shown me whatever it was that I was supposed to be out here to see.

God said nothing on my walk. I heard no voices, I saw no vision, there were no burning bushes or angels or anything out of the ordinary that showed up. This was another grand waste of time. I turned around and went home and fell into bed, exhausted.

The next day, I went about my work day, numb. I was not excited about my current job. It paid the bills, but it wasn't a good fit for my skills, and because of that, I felt like it was a poor use of both my time and company resources for me to be in the role. At least it was a remote job. That meant that I wasn't tied to Arizona, or to anyplace at all for that matter. I remembered my mental note from the night before, and on my lunch break from work, I pulled up Zillow, and I typed in Twain Harte, just to see what was available.

At the top of the page, the first house that popped up was a new listing, and it looked nice. The house backed up to "the ditch," a term that local residents used to refer to a system of man-made water channels and elevated flumes that ran through the woods. In most places where the ditch was at ground level, it really looked more like a stream than a man-made conduit. The ditch also had hiking trails that meandered along the length of the channels for most of its seventy-two-mile system. I had always thought that it would be nice to live along the ditch.

I kept scrolling to see what the rest of the Twain Harte real estate market looked like. It wasn't a long list. Most of the houses that I saw were either too small, too expensive, didn't have a garage, or needed a lot of work. After my last remodel, I was not eager to jump back into another project house. But the house on the ditch had recently been renovated. It had a two-car garage, it was the right size, and it was in my price range. I liked what the owners had done with it, and the listing even said that the owner would consider selling many of the furnishings. This appealed to me, as my Arizona-style furnishings would not be a good fit for Twain Harte. This house checked all of the boxes, and there was nothing else on the market that checked even most of them. I hadn't planned on doing anything right away, I was just going to have a look online, but the more I looked at this house, the more certain I became that this was the house for me.

So, I just went for it. I picked up the phone and I called one of the real estate agents from the office where I had worked when I had lived in Twain Harte. Her name was Betsy, and in addition to being a former colleague, Betsy had also been a good friend. Betsy and I agreed that with so little decent inventory on the market, if we waited until I could travel to Twain Harte, there was a good chance that the house on the ditch would be gone.

I gave Betsy her marching orders: Get me under contract on that house before the weekend. After a bit of back-and-forth, we were under contract within forty-eight hours – for the house and for all of the furnishings. Every rug, every lamp, all of the art and accessories, and even every houseplant would be left in the home. All that I had to do was to show up with my personal items and my pets.

Christy worked her magic on getting my Arizona house under contract just as quickly. With my recent remodel, the house showed extremely well, and after only one day of showings, we had nineteen offers. I sold my house for well above list price to buyers who were new to the country and who were moving here with nothing but their clothing. They bought all of my furnishings and décor as well. All of the parties on both ends of both deals got exactly what they wanted and needed.

Over the next month, I packed up my belongings into boxes while watching through my front window as my sister did the same. She had moved equally quickly on her arrangements, and she would be headed to Texas a few weeks after I left for Twain Harte. Judie and I spent our last month of dinners together talking about our plans for our lives in our new towns and how we would miss each other but how we were both so grateful for this season that we had had together.

I had more conversations with God as well. I didn't know what He was up to, but I eventually resigned myself to the fact that I was just going to have to trust Him. What choice did I have? I had nothing left to fall back on. I had nowhere else to turn. If this was all part of some plan, I was just going to have to go along for the ride and find out what it was as we went.

Just over a month after that fateful conversation with my sister, in the wee hours of a hot Arizona summer morning, I loaded my pets and my last few items into my car, took a long last look at my house and at my sister's house across the street, put the car in gear, and set out to drive the 741 miles straight through to my new house in Twain Harte, California. Larry would be meeting me at the other end to welcome me to my new home, and I was looking forward to being greeted by at least one face that I knew. After fourteen-plus hours on the road with multiple stops for dog walking, cat box scooping, fast-food, and fuel, I pulled up to the house on the ditch late in the afternoon of what would have been my parents' sixty-fifth wedding anniversary.

Twain Harte was beautiful. The house was exactly as it had looked in the pictures. My new home was surrounded by a mix of healthy pines, cedars, and oaks. My front deck had a lovely view overlooking a grassy meadow and a pond beyond the trees, and the steps of my back door led right out to the ditch trail, where I could walk alongside fresh, running water. I could see myself having many more conversations with God during walks along the ditch. If I had to be lost, this was a good place to be lost in.

One afternoon, as I was sorting through boxes and shuttling items between the house, the garage, and the shed, my dog wandered off. My dog was not a runner, but I did need to track her down. My dog hadn't gone far, she had just wandered over to the neighbor's yard in search of her new friend – a similar dog who lived in the yard adjacent to mine. As I walked across the neighbor's yard to collect my dog, a woman opened up a window from inside.

"Hi, are you our new neighbor?" she called.

"Yeah, I just moved in. I'm sorry about my dog. She wandered off. I hope she wasn't bothering you."

"Oh no, not at all. Hold on, I'll come out!"

My neighbor came outside and introduced herself as Michelle. We chatted a little bit about dogs and houses and families and Twain Harte. Then Michelle said, "Hey, I don't know if you're looking for a church in town, but if you are, I'd love to invite you to check out mine."

I thought about Michelle's invitation for a minute. This was the type of situation where I would usually either say "no" right away or give some type of non-committal response in order to get out of the conversation. But Michelle seemed really nice, and her invitation felt like just that: an invitation. Not a sales pitch. Not a guilt trip. Just a simple invitation.

"Sure, why not?" I heard myself say to my own surprise, and Michelle and I exchanged information.

That evening, as I was sitting on my front deck enjoying the cool, fresh air, I chatted with God.

"Church, God? Really? I haven't been around churchy people for thirty years. Not since the ministry. I haven't been to a service in an actual church building for even longer than that. This is really weird, God. What are You up to?"

I thought about the last time that I had attended church services in a church building. Other than the occasional Christmas or Easter service that I had attended to appease my parents, the last time that I had attended a regular church service was when I was married to my first husband, Luke, the Lutheran church youth leader, during the time that I was wrapped up in that mess at the brokerage. The Lutheran church would serve communion one Sunday per month. I still remember kneeling around the alter in that church, taking communion, and having only one prayer for God: "Don't give up on me." That was the only prayer of my own that I ever prayed in that church, and I prayed that prayer every single time that I took communion.

"Is this why I'm here in Twain Harte, God? Is this why you brought me to this particular house on the ditch? Is there something or someone in that church that you want me to meet, or some message that you want me to hear? Surely You don't think that I would actually go to a church, like on a regular basis, do You? Those churchy people would eat me for lunch!"

The next morning was a Sunday. I thought about Michelle's invitation. I went online. Michelle's church had a website. I checked it out. Based on the website, the church didn't look overly cringe-worthy, but it was still a church, and it would be full of churchy people whom I was sure could not wait to barf Jesus all over the new person and then tell me about how everything I had ever done or thought was wrong and that I needed to repent right there on the spot or I was surely going straight to hell. Oh yeah, that sounded like a rousing good time.

The website had videos of past church services. Maybe I should check out one of those first. See what I was getting myself into before I actually showed up. If it was too weird, I could just not go. I clicked on a random video. It started with music. The music was actually pretty good. I made myself a cup of coffee and sat down on my couch and waited for the music to be over so that I could see what really went on in that place. The music kept going and going and going. It went on for a whole hour! Was this a church service or a concert? It couldn't be a concert; everybody in the whole church was singing.

Finally, the message started. The first thing that I noticed was that a woman was preaching. I had not seen that in a church before. There were lots of women leaders in the ministry that I had been part of, but in the churches that I had been in, all of the leaders had been men. The second thing that I noticed was that this woman was on fire! She was extremely passionate about what she was sharing. It wasn't the stoic, boring stuff that I had endured when I was a kid, but it also wasn't the pompous, holier-than-thou stuff that I had seen from televangelists who had always seemed more interested in collecting donations for faraway places than actually helping anybody who was right in front of them. What I was watching was not a performance. This woman clearly cared.

I was curious. I watched another video. This time, it was a man preaching. A great big, bald, tough guy who looked like somebody that I wouldn't want to meet in a dark alley. He was on fire too! With the same heart. I watched another one. And another one. After binge watching six straight services in a row, a couple more things stood out. One was that nobody asked for money. Not one time. I think somebody mentioned information about the different ways that you could give if you wanted to, but that was it. Another thing that stood out was that, just like the ministry that I had been part of, these people were actually teaching what was happening in the Bible in context. They weren't just pulling out random verses and then giving their personal perspectives.

But the main thing that I noticed is that they were all talking about love. They weren't spewing judgment and condemnation all over everybody. Just like my conversation with Michelle, the people preaching and teaching were extending an invitation to know more. That was it. Take it or don't, and if you don't, we love you anyway. That wasn't too scary. I figured maybe I could go there one time, maybe the next Sunday, and check it out. If it was weird, I would just leave.

"How does that sound, God?"

God nodded, and I think I caught a hint of a smile.

CHAPTER TWENTY-FOUR

Crickets

Over the next few weeks, I kept meaning to go and check out Michelle's church, but I kept finding reasons not to do it. I was still getting things put away in my house. I was figuring out what to do with my career situation. I wanted to hike the ditch trail up to the feeder reservoir. Besides, I could just watch the services online from the safety of my own home, where no churchy people would pounce on me with daggers of judgment from behind a veil of feigned sweetness. Yes, watching from home would be much safer.

As I continued adjusting to my new life in Twain Harte, every day that I spent in the misfit role of my reassigned job felt wrong. The company was paying me an awful lot of money, and I didn't feel like I was adding much value, which felt both demoralizing and ethically questionable. I was an entrepreneur at heart, and I had found ways to exercise those muscles in my last several corporate roles as an intrapreneur – leading transformational initiatives and launching new products from within a company. The job that I was in now was in an intrapreneurial part of the company, but my assigned role was more on the compliance side than on the innovation side. It was almost harder for me to sit that close to the real action and observe, having no meaningful leadership role, it than it would have been for me to be removed from the action altogether.

I took stock of my situation. Ever since I had left the ministry and joined the corporate world, I had always yearned to get back to having a business of my own. I had had a taste of it with my own law firm, but I hadn't had that firm long enough to really build it up, and it probably wasn't the right long term business for me anyway. I thought about my conversations with God and about having the heart of a servant. I had to take care to focus on the right question. The question wasn't: What could I do where I could really shine? When I had begun to get caught back up in that, God had taken that role away from me after only three weeks. No, the question that I needed to ask myself was: What was I uniquely well-suited and well-positioned to do that could be of great service to others?

Coaching high-potential leadership talent had been on my mind over the past few months. I had worked with some really good coaches myself, and I had considered the idea of coaching after I had left my role as company president. I had certainly been through enough personal and professional transitions to know where a lot of the potholes were. Especially after God had pointed out some of the biggest ones out to me. Maybe I could help other people by using what I had learned. I had mentored plenty of people over the course of my career. How different could coaching be?

I decided to find out. I did some research on coach training, and I was surprised to learn that the coaching industry was entirely unregulated and widely fragmented. Anybody who wanted to call themselves a certified coach could obtain a certification that was endorsed by the leading industry organization simply by taking a three-day course over a long weekend. That wasn't very much training, but I figured it would get my feet wet, and if it happened to come with a certification, I wasn't going to turn that down.

The course was very interesting. Coaching and mentoring were not the same thing. Mentoring is more about imparting your own knowledge, experience, wisdom, and connections to help another person to get ahead, whereas coaching is more about providing tools and asking the right questions to help another person to grow from the inside out. I liked the coaching idea. I would need more than three days of training to do it well, but I could do that.

I made a plan. The whole next year, 2024, would be a year of preparation for me. I knew how to launch a business. I just needed to learn how to be a good coach. I would read and I would study under coaches of my own. I would practice with people who knew that they were being practiced on until I was confident that I was actually helping them. I would put together a business plan, and I would get everything lined up so that at the end of 2024, I could leave my misfit job and open a business of my own. I had something to be excited about again. This was going to be great!

Before I moved forward with my plan, I figured that I had better check in with God. I had been taking regular afternoon walks along the ditch, so on one of my walks, I ran my idea by Him. I assured Him that I would approach this idea with the heart of a servant. After laying out my whole plan, I received no feedback from God at all. Crickets. At least that meant no negative feedback. No red flags so far. I figured that if God didn't want me to move forward, He would let me know somehow.

And then I wondered… Maybe God would have something to say about my plan if I showed up at church like I had said that I would. I supposed that I could go just the one time. Check it out. What was the worst thing that could happen? Hmmm… To stay on the safe side, I decided to leave that last question in the rhetorical category.

The next Sunday morning, I set my alarm. I got up, I got showered, I got ready, and I made myself a lunch. On the videos that I had watched, there had been an announcement every week that everyone was invited to the church's fellowship hall after service to have lunch together. If I were going to go to this church just the one time, I was going to go for the whole experience. I drove to the church. I parked. I was early. I hadn't wanted to draw any extra attention to myself by walking in late, but I didn't want to walk in early either. If I walked in early, I might have to talk to people. That would be way too scary. No, I wanted to walk in right on time. I would wait in my car until one minute before the service was scheduled to start.

When the time to go in arrived, I could not get out of that car. This was ridiculous. What was I afraid of? These people might not welcome me and my messy history, but it's not like I was going to catch on fire just by crossing the threshold of a church. It was just one service. One and done. I could do this.

I managed to muster two seconds worth of courage – just enough to throw open the car door. Once the door was open, I stepped out of the car. With both feet now planted on the ground, I looked up. There were people. People who saw me get out of the car. It was too late now to get back into the car and drive away. If I did that, I would surely never return. I closed the door and locked the car. I walked across the parking lot and into the church. I sat down in the very last row. As close to the door as I could possibly get. I had learned that from the day that I had walked into room 150 in the music building. Sit near the exit. And just like that day in room 150, I tried to be as invisible as possible.

I remember almost nothing about the church service that day. I have no idea who preached, or what the message was. I was too focused on trying to be inconspicuous and hoping not to catch on fire. I do remember people being very nice, but not creepy-pushy-nice. I also remember following along with the herd as people walked from the church to the fellowship hall after the service. Just like I had followed along with the rest of the sopranos from room 150 to the sectional rehearsal room.

I had no idea where to sit in the fellowship hall, so I just plunked myself down at a table that had a bunch of other lunch bags already there. I figured that sitting with people would be less conspicuous than sitting by myself. As the owners of the lunch bags trickled in to claim their chairs and the table began to fill up, I realized that I was the only person sitting at that table who was over thirty years old. I was old enough to be everyone's mother! Apparently, I had chosen a seat at the young adults table. I didn't dare to move. I just stayed right there, glued to my seat, and I chatted with the young adults, who were also very welcoming and not creepy-pushy. After lunch, I thanked the young adults for their conversation. Then I stood up, and I beelined for the exit as stealthily as possible. Back towards the safety of my car.

When I finally made it home and walked in through my front door, I collapsed into a chair. I felt like I had been holding my breath for hours! I wiggled my spiritual fingers and toes. I hadn't caught on fire, so that was one good thing. Nobody had yelled at me. Nobody had judged me. And nobody had been weird. Granted, I hadn't gone into any depth about myself, but the whole day had actually been surprisingly uneventful. I had questions for God about that. I took a walk on the ditch trail.

"Okay, God, I went. I showed up, just like I said I would. Nothing happened. Nothing bad happened, but nothing really happened at all. What was I supposed to get out of that?"

More crickets. God said nothing. Was that it? I showed up to church one time, and God was done talking to me? Was this His whole plan? Was He handing me off to churchy people so that He could go talk to somebody else now? I guess I had been taking up a lot of His time. I really had been a royal pain in His backside for quite a long while now. And I hadn't been very polite when I had talked with Him. He probably had more important things to do now that He had handed me off. I wasn't sure how I felt about that, but I kind of deserved it. However, I also wasn't too sure that I wanted to go back to the church again. That would be a big leap. At some point, I would get found out, and I was sure that all of those nice, churchy people wouldn't want me around after that.

I remembered that there had been mention during the service of an opportunity to have coffee with a couple of the pastors on Wednesday nights. It was a time set aside specifically for new people to go and ask questions in a small, intimate setting. Maybe I should go to a Wednesday night. That seemed less intimidating. Also, I could just dump everything out, all at once, and see if they kicked me out. That's what I would do. That would settle this once and for all.

"What do you think about that idea, God?"

Crickets.

I didn't go to the coffee house that Wednesday night, or the next one. I needed to take a breath, and I was kind of waiting to see if I might hear from God. Maybe I could get out of the Wednesday night idea if He would just speak to me directly again.

Besides, I had a business to plan, and I was getting excited! I had ordered several books on coaching and had devoured every one of them. I had begun coaching a couple of practice clients. I had signed up with two different programs to get coaching for myself on the ins and outs of this particular kind of business. And I had started following coaches that I liked online in order to get a feel for how they ran their own businesses.

The more that I read and the more that I learned, the more that my business mind began to kick in. Coaching individual clients would be a fine start, but it was not a scalable business model. The economics would be just like a regular job: trading my time for a set dollar amount. Once my schedule filled up, I would be capped out on earnings. That business model would also limit the number of people that I could serve. In order to help the next client, an existing client would have to get out of the way. God already knew how I felt about limits. There had to be a better way. How would I scale my business?

I read a bunch more books and listened to different coaches about how they had scaled their own businesses. There were all kinds of ways to scale a coaching business. From group coaching to book publishing to courses to blogs to podcasts to speaking engagements to corporate clients, there was no shortage of avenues to reach more people and to earn more money in the process.

Most of the books that I read encouraged setting a revenue goal and then mapping out a path to get there. That made good business sense, and those types of goals had always motivated me to drive to exceed them. The bar that a lot of coaches suggested setting felt quite low to me, by about a factor of ten. I knew that I could do better. So, I set myself a revenue target that felt like a stretch goal, but achievable, and I retooled my plan to get there. If I could execute on that plan – and I was confident that I could – I would achieve my first revenue target in a few short years, and I would 10x that number a few years later. Now that felt like a real business!

With all of my flow charts and calculations spread out across my kitchen table, I stepped back out on the ditch trail, and I ran my new and improved plan by God. Still crickets. I got no comment from God whatsoever. That felt oddly disconcerting. I had gone through decades in business, achieving and exceeding every goal that was set before me without even once seeking any input from God. Yet now that I had started speaking with Him again, I felt like I needed His blessing to move forward with a perfectly good business plan that I knew full well how to execute, and He was nowhere to be found.

I really felt like I needed to hear from God before moving forward. Maybe I should go to a Wednesday night coffee with the pastors. Maybe God would have a message for me there.

CHAPTER TWENTY-FIVE

Wednesdays with Pastors

Wednesday evening came around, and once again, I got into my car and headed up the hill toward the church. The meeting with the pastors would be held at the coffee house nearby. I arrived a few minutes early, and I saw that the coffee house was closed. Hmmm… maybe I had gotten the information wrong somehow. But there were a couple of cars in the parking lot, so I tried the door, and I found it unlocked. I opened the door and walked in. There were four pastors inside. Four! I knew that they were all pastors, because I recognized them from the website and from the videos. I introduced myself, and one of the pastors offered to make me a cup of coffee herself. The espresso machine was fired up, she said. I could have anything that I wanted. That sounded great! She made me a delicious decaf latte.

Other than those four pastors and me, there were no other people in the whole coffee house. The venue was indeed closed. They were using it on Wednesday evenings specifically for the purpose of pastors having coffee with whomever wanted to drop by. No one else dropped by. I was seriously outnumbered. I was going to be alone in a room with four pastors for two hours!

I should have been massively intimidated. Instead, I took the opportunity to get to know them, and I shared a little bit about myself as well. I didn't dump everything out all at once like I had planned, but I shared enough to watch and to gauge their reaction. They listened. I saw no alarm on anyone's face. We just talked matter-of-factly about everything that I brought up. History, questions, plans for the future. All were fair game, and none were met with any kind of negative reaction. In fact, quite the opposite happened. Every question was asked with genuine curiosity, and every response and every answer that they gave me was based in love.

After only a couple of hours, these pastors were beginning to feel comfortable, almost like family. I don't know how it happened, but I got the sense that I might have somehow stumbled into to a new dad and a new mom and a bonus sister and brother as well. I wasn't sure that I trusted that sense, but it sure did feel good. Good enough that I would go back the next Wednesday, and the one after that, peeling back more and more layers each time. I remembered what God had said: "Allow others to reflect My love back to you and to help you in your times of need." These seemed like good people for me to start with.

Meanwhile, I continued to develop my business plan. The plan was becoming more and more concrete. Chronologically, it would start with a book. I could write the book during 2024 while I was still working in my misfit job. The book would shine a light on the trend of women leaders leaving the corporate workplace in record numbers, and it would provide a framework both for the women themselves and for the corporations where they worked to address this trend from within, rather than having to part ways with one another. The book would be the first piece of a marketing funnel that I would build to channel potential executive and corporate clients into my business. The book would be followed by a podcast, a blog, and speaking engagements, all feeding into a program of courses, coaching, and community that in turn would feed into each other. I really liked this plan. It would be a lot of work, but it felt doable.

It was time to get started on the first piece of the funnel: writing the book. I had never written a book before, so I read a few books about how to write this kind of book, and then I sat down to begin my own writing.

Nothing came.

I wasn't too concerned. I would work a bit more on my business plan and then come back to the book.

I worked on my plan some more. I came back to the book.

Nothing came.

Hmmm. Apparently, I needed more than a few books' worth of instruction to learn how to do this. I enrolled in a book-writing boot-camp. The course was great! It laid out exactly what I needed to do. I was ready now! I set out to execute.

Nothing came.

What was going on? I had written all my life. I had had legal articles picked up for publication in academic journals. I had written reports and press releases and marketing copy for a living. Writer's block was not something that happened to me.

Maybe I needed a better outline. I knew the book that I wanted to write. So, I outlined it in great detail, in much the same way that I had created outlines for my published academic articles.

Nothing came.

Research! That's what was missing. I had planned to pull research as needed as I went along, but I realized that if I completed all of the research first, it would better inform the trajectory of the book. I did tons and tons of research. Now I was ready to go!

Nothing came.

I left the stacks of research piled on my kitchen table, and I set back out on the ditch trail to take this predicament up with God. "God, what is happening? I've always been a writer. Why can't I write a single word of this book?"

Crickets.

As I was working through all of this, I continued my Wednesday night conversations with the pastors. Sometimes, other people came on Wednesday nights, but often times, it was just me and the pastors. Selfishly, I enjoyed those nights the most, because they gave me the opportunity to have really candid, uncensored conversations. On one such Wednesday, I finally dumped out the last of my ballast. Every bit of my history was on the table now, including my history with sexuality. If they were ever going to turn me away, this would be it.

They didn't turn me away. Instead, after fully hearing me out, we just talked about my journey. I shared with them how I had now come to understand that my quest for love had never really been about sexuality. How I had come to realize that I had been searching everywhere for love in vain, looking in every corner, seeking from people the kind of intimate love that only God can give. We talked a lot about how finger-pointing and name-calling by Christians only served to drive away from the church those who needed God's love the most. People like me. To my great relief, the whole conversation was grounded in love and compassion, and without a hint of judgment.

I also shared that I was in the middle of a transformational time in my life. I described how I had recently dived into deep mental and emotional waters to explore who I really am and to understand and leave behind patterns of behavior that were destructive to me. I shared about my conversations with God, and about how I was trying to approach planning my new business with the heart of a servant. I also shared that this journey that I was on was an ongoing process, and that some of the water was still murky to me. The pastors listened and provided gentle guidance and some suggested reading, but they didn't think it was weird that I was talking with God, and they didn't usurp the process.

While we were on the topic of my dive into the water, I had a question about water baptism. The pastors had given me a series of books to help me to regain my bearings after thirty years away from God. Baptism had been covered in one of them, but it had been covered differently from how I had previously experienced it. I had been baptized as a young teen in the Lutheran church with a few dribbles of water and a napkin and not much of an understanding about what was going on. But on the day that I had binge-watched six church services, I had seen a video of a baptism where the people had actually been immersed fully underwater. I was curious. What was that all about?

What one of the pastors explained to me about baptism filled in a lot of the conversations that I had been having with God. It seemed that the reason that I kept making the same mistakes over and over again was not because I was any worse of a human being than anyone else, but because humans are imperfect by nature. Once the first humans had disobeyed God, the rest of us were bound to follow suit. To this day, there is no mechanism by which any of us can perfect our own human nature. However, there is a mechanism by which we can trade up.

This was not a question of salvation; that had already happened for me decades ago, whether I acted like it or not (and I most certainly had not). It also wasn't a question of spiritual baptism. Both spiritual cleansing and being filled with the Holy Spirit had happened for me decades earlier also. This was about something else. This was a heart question. Through water baptism, God had provided a way that I could trade up to a new heart. Instead of being doomed to constantly mess up, I could ditch my old, stony heart and choose to live with a new, soft heart of love.

I was all ears as the pastor continued. When the first humans blew it, their transgression came with serious consequences. Not only did it come with a death sentence for themselves and for all future generations, it also came with the consequence that all future generations would not have the capacity to keep themselves from screwing up. Human nature was broken from then on.

However, God did promise that he would send somebody to fix this situation for the rest of us. The price would be hefty, but because God loved us, He would take care of it. The person that He would send to fix this situation for us would have some pretty tall orders. The person would have to live perfectly, then get tortured, then be brutally executed, then go down into hell to pay the ransom to redeem us, and then come back through here again before going back up to heaven. By one person somehow pulling all of that off, the rest of us would get a new deal with God, including the option to trade in our old, flawed heart for a brand new one.

The question was: Who could actually pull that off? The challenge was so great that nobody on earth had the ability to do it. The only one who stood any chance at pulling all of that off was God's own Son. What kind of love must God have had for us to send His only Son to do that terrible job? You would think that everyone would have been cheering Jesus on the whole way as He ran that perfect race for us, all the way through to the finish. But most people didn't, and most people still don't. There is no requirement that anyone does. There was no requirement that I did. But the job was done, the price was paid, and if I wanted to, I could take part in the reward. A new heart was mine for the taking, and there was nothing that I needed to do to earn it.

"What does all of that have to do with going under water?" I asked.

The pastor explained that when we are water baptized, we choose to accept Christ's death, burial, and resurrection as our own. The waters of baptism are symbolic of the grave. We bury both the person that we used to be and the influence of the world system in the water, and we leave those things there. It is a complete separation between our old self and our new self. By partaking of Christ's death and burial in that way, as we rise up from the water, we partake in His resurrection also, and we walk in newness of life. By operation of water baptism, we are no longer powerless over our own actions. We now have the ability to choose not to screw up. The choice, of course, is still ours, but now we can actually make that choice.

That was a lot of information for me to digest. I was going to have to think about that for a while. I had also never heard a lot of what the pastor was talking about, and I was going to have to go and read about those things in the Bible for myself.

As I drove home that Wednesday evening, I thought about the struggles that I had been having with writing my book and with planning my business, and I realized that one of the things that the pastor had said was true: I just couldn't manage to keep from slipping back into my old ways. I was still trying to do everything myself. My business plan was *my* plan. Somewhere along the way, I had lost focus on service, and I had rotated back to focusing on scale, focusing on money, building something outwardly great and praiseworthy, living up to the standards of others. *Choose your God.* Without even realizing it, I had slipped from a well-intentioned idea back to choosing myself. Again.

CHAPTER TWENTY-SIX

I Am

In the ensuing weeks, as I took stock of my situation, I was really in a pickle. I was still working in my misfit job, but I didn't feel like I was doing right by either myself or my employer. I had already made some major financial investments in the business that I was planning to start, and I had a strong sense that I was headed in the right general direction, but I just couldn't get the focus dialed in. Every time that I tried to force clear goals, the focus of those goals tended more toward building something outwardly impressive than toward service of others. I continued to forge ahead with the pieces that I knew would be needed for the business no matter which direction it took, while at the same time I was striving to get clarity on the rest.

On one ordinary day, as I took my afternoon walk along the ditch following a long and marginally productive meeting at the end of a long and marginally productive workday, I heard from God for the first time in months.

"Oh, there you are!" I exclaimed. I was really happy to hear His voice.

God spoke. "Go now."

"What?" I waited for more.

"Go now."

There was no more. But I was pretty sure that I understood what God was saying, and it terrified me. I had planned for 2024 to be a year of preparation to start my business, which would launch in 2025. I would stay in my misfit job through most or all of 2024, doing the best that I could to add value and to leave the business unit better off than when I found it. The job paid very well, and keeping that income flowing for the rest of the year would set me up nicely to launch my business. This timeline would also allow me to get all of the preparations done before launch so that the business could start generating revenue almost immediately. Pulling that trigger now, ten months ahead of schedule, especially while my business plan was still in flux, made no financial sense. It made no business sense. It made no logical sense. It made no kind of sense at all.

I had a choice to make. Was I going to put my trust in my own logic? Was I going to take the safe route and not pull that trigger until I was sure that I had all my financial ducks in a row and knew exactly where the business was going? Was I going to rely on my own understanding? Was I still holding on to a remnant of that boat tether? Or was I going to put all of my trust in God and go now? *Choose your God.*

I inhaled a long breath and gulped down my fear, and I committed right there and then to go now. With that commitment, I was finally completely untethered. I kept looking up toward the surface, watching the bottom of my wrecked boat it as it drifted out of sight. It was the most disorienting feeling that I have ever had. I was totally undefined.

As I walked back to my house, I asked God to give me a sign. Some kind of sign that I had heard Him correctly. That I hadn't just imagined what I had heard or misunderstood what He had said. I spent the rest of that evening suspended underwater in a feeling of complete sensory deprivation. I had nothing from the world to grab hold of, and I didn't know where I was going. My commitment to go now was made, but I sure would feel a lot more comfortable if there was some way that I could be sure that I had made the right decision.

The next morning, I stood at my kitchen window with a cup of coffee, looking out over the front deck, and I observed a curious sight. A couple of the potted plants that I had inherited when I bought my house had died during the winter freezes. I should have covered them or brought them indoors, but they were well past saving now – or so I had thought. Both of those plants had budded overnight. Even if they hadn't actually died in the freezes as I had thought, they shouldn't have been budding until April or May. This was early February! There was snow on the ground, and nighttime temperatures had been dropping below freezing all week. Could this be my sign? I will never know for sure, but it was enough for me to muster the courage to act on the decision that I had made the night before. I tendered my resignation to my employer. The money faucet would soon be turned off.

I was now all in with God. In addition to spending Wednesday evenings at the coffee house with the pastors, I had also been attending Sunday services – something that I never could have imagined even a few short months earlier. I had studied the books that the pastors had given me, but more importantly, I had read the things that they had talked about in the Bible itself until I was comfortable that I had understood them.

I was also becoming more and more clear on the difference between religion and faith. Religion has the potential to do a tremendous amount of harm. So many people have been hurt by churches and by Christians, whether intentionally or not. I would like to think that most of the hurt is inflicted unintentionally, but even the best of intentions, alone, don't change the outcome, and the results can be devastating. They sure were for me. I didn't want to live a life of religion. I didn't want to live a life in judgement and condemnation of myself or of others. I just wanted to live a life of love and grace. I wanted to choose the God of love, and to keep choosing love every single day.

I decided that I needed to get baptized. I wanted that new heart that the pastor had taught me about. I wanted the ability to be able to make choices based in love. I wanted that complete separation from the old me so that I could choose to live with the heart of a servant. It was time for me to come up from the water.

When baptism day arrived, Larry accompanied me to church that morning. Larry was a member of a different church, the same one that my parents had attended when they were alive, but Larry wanted to be there with me on my special day. In a way, Larry was standing in as a surrogate for my parents, and it warmed my heart to have him there.

When my turn to get baptized came, I was ready. One of the pastors spoke over me, declaring what was happening, and the next thing that I knew, helping hands lowered me fully into the water. I don't remember anything about being under the water, but when those same helping hands lifted me back up from the water, the feeling that I had in that moment was indescribable. It was hard to tell how much of the water dripping from my face had come from below and how much of it was coming from inside of me, but somehow, everything felt new. I had gone from feeling totally undefined to being totally defined by God. When I came up from the water, I knew who I was, and I knew Whose I was.

I am!

After my water baptism, I walked around for the next several days in a daze. I felt like my whole being was vibrating on a different level. I didn't fully know what to make of all that had happened or what would come next. I was just trying to be present with God in the moment and to listen.

In the weeks and months that followed, I took many walks along the ditch with God. I thought about all that He and I had talked about.

I thought about music, how much joy it had brought me, and how I might invite music back into my life. I had learned of an opportunity to sing the chorus of Beethoven's Ninth Symphony at San José State University that summer. It was just a community sing, but it would get my feet wet, and it would be fondly nostalgic to rehearse in room 150 again after all these years. I signed up.

I thought about the many poor choices that I had made in my life. I thought about the role that alcohol had played in nearly all of them. I had already made the decision shortly after moving to Twain Harte that alcohol was not serving me well, and I had stopped drinking altogether. I figured that was just easier than having to discern every time when enough was enough. It occurred to me now that after all of these months of not drinking, I really didn't miss it. I was glad to have that stumbling block out of my life.

I thought about how I had sought love everywhere. How I had looked in every corner and under every rock for something that was right in front of me the whole time. How I had placed expectations on the shoulders of others, rather than picking up their burdens and carrying them on my own shoulders. I thought about how I needed to be intentional now about looking for ways to give love, every day.

I thought about how I had tried so hard all my life to prove to the world that I was worthy. That I wasn't a weak, sickly little child that nobody wanted on their team. I contrasted that with the family name that I now knew I had. I was a child of God! I had all of the power and authority that came with that family name. I had not earned it, it was nothing to be prideful about, but it was comforting, and it also came with a great responsibility to serve.

I thought about my parents. What wonderful parents that God had given me. How they had raised me in the church, just as they had promised, and how they had done their best to guide me in the best way that they knew how. I thought about how they weren't perfect, but how much I had loved them anyway, and how much they had loved me, despite my own imperfections.

And I thought about the little slip of paper that I had found in Mom's wallet that now lived in mine. How the words that I had been carrying around described the heart of a servant:

My Daily Commitment

Today, dear God, I am available. Please make me usable and help me to be Christ to my family, to someone in need, and to every life I touch this day.

One afternoon, as I was walking along the trail with God, taking in the pine trees and the singing birds and the flowing water running alongside me, I thought back to those lovely, midweek, summer days at Lake Pillsbury. Those days where, as a child, I would lie out on the empty dock, staring up at the clouds in the sky and marveling at all that had to come together just right to create such a planet as this where we all could live. Even then, I knew that all of this must have some kind of purpose. That each one of us must be here on some kind of assignment. I still didn't have all of the details of my own assignment, but I knew for certain that it would be based in the words on that slip of paper that I had found in my mother's wallet. On the heart of a servant. I knew who I was, and I knew Whose I was, and I knew that I had love to serve up to the world. I turned around and headed back down the trail toward home. It was time for me to get busy serving. *Go now.*

Epilogue

Shortly after my water baptism, I sat down again to try to write my book. Still, nothing came. I didn't understand. I had a new heart! I knew who I was! God had instructed me to go now, and I had gone. I had an even stronger sense that a book was where I was supposed to start. I felt like even the process of writing a book would give me clarity on what I was supposed to do next. So why could I not write even a single word?

"What am I missing, God?"

God answered. "You're writing the wrong book."

"What?"

I don't know why I kept asking God to repeat Himself every time that he told me something. I made a mental note to work on that.

"You're writing the wrong book."

"But God, this book is part of my business plan! Chronologically, it's the first piece. Like the first domino in a line. If I don't push the first domino over, none of the rest of them will fall."

"Exactly."

"So… oh, wow. Oh my." This whole conversation was going to have some pretty serious implications for my business. I would process that in a minute. But right now, I had God engaged, and I was not going to let Him go before I understood what He was saying. God hadn't said not to write a book. He had said that I was writing the *wrong* one. That implied that there was a right one. Which meant that I was still supposed to write a book.

"So then, what book do You want me to write?"

God answered. "Write your story."

"My story? Who is going to want to read that? I am not that interesting, God. I'm not famous. I don't have industry-leading business accomplishments. I haven't climbed Mount Everest or through-hiked the Appalachian Trail. I don't have the kind of sensational story of overcoming impossible odds that people like to read about. I've pretty much mostly just screwed up, God. I am remarkably unremarkable."

"Write your story."

God must have been getting tired of me arguing as much as He must have been getting tired of me acting like I was hard of hearing.

"Okay, God," I surrendered. And that was the end of that conversation.

I filed away all of my notes and research from the book that I had originally planned to write, and I paused all of the wheels that were in motion on my business. I didn't throw any of those things out. God hadn't said to do that. He had simply instructed me to write my story, and to do it now.

Once my work-in-progress was stacked away on my mental shelf for safekeeping, I sat down to start an outline for what would now be a very different book. I made all kinds of notes about my various life experiences. What had happened. How I had responded. What I had learned. I filled up notebook after notebook and emptied nearly as many boxes of Kleenex. When I had finished dumping all of that out, I couldn't even draft so much as an outline for the new book. Getting this book organized was even harder than the book before!

But God had instructed me to write it, so I asked Him, "God, how should I organize this? What should I write about? Where do I even begin?"

God answered. "Just start writing. I'll help you."

Just start writing? I asked that question in my head. I was trying to be more intentional about not arguing with God or asking Him to repeat himself. Other than the writing that I had done in my journals,

I had never just free-written anything of consequence before. I was skeptical that this type of process would result in anything more than purposeless rambling. Nevertheless, I did as I was told. I opened up a blank Word document on my laptop, and I started writing. I started with the only thing that I was sure of. "This isn't the book I was going to write…," I began.

From there, the book just flowed. Up to this moment, I hadn't been able to write so much as a single word. Now, the words were coming as fast as I could get them down. Page after page. Chapter after chapter. First hundreds of words per day, then thousands. I would start each day with a little prayer: *God, where are we going with this today?* At the end of each day, I would look back over the day's work to find that what I had written was practically unrecognizable in comparison with what I had thought I was going to write. I kept going. I wrote all day, every day, six days per week. I felt an unexplained sense of urgency. God had said to go now for a reason, even if I didn't know what that reason was. By the end of three months, I had a completed draft.

The book that you hold in your hands is that book. As I write these very words, God still hasn't told me why I'm writing it or who it is for. It's possible that this book is just for me. The process of writing it has helped me to fully immerse myself into the water. A few dribbles on the surface weren't going to have much transformational value. I had to dive deep in order to rise up from the water and to fully walk in the newness of life. Writing this book has helped me to do that.

So yes, writing this book was definitely for me. But I suspect that there may be a nugget or two in here for someone else also. Maybe there's something in here for you. I hope so.

May God bless you with His abundant love. And may you find your own true identity in your own journey into and up from the water.

Afterword

Dear friend,

Writing this book has been an unexpected privilege along an unlikely journey. I've done my best to write this book with the heart of a servant. If you have found something in this book that speaks to you, I'd love to hear about it. I would love to know what touched you. I'd love to hear where you are in your own journey through the water. And if you're feeling like you could use a hand to help you to fully immerse and then rise up from the water, I would be honored to lend you my hand in love. I invite you to scan the QR code below to share your comments or to reach out.

In addition, if you would like to have a little card for your own wallet that contains the words from the slip of paper that I found in my mother's wallet and now carry in mine, simply scan the QR code below, and I'll be happy to mail a card to you. It is my gift to you. Actually, it's a gift from my mom. And if we're all being really honest, it is a gift from God to all of us.

Acknowledgments

Heartfelt thanks to my family, both born and chosen, who provided support and gentle feedback as I was writing this book; especially Judie, Cindy, Genny, and Clyde. Thank you also to my friends and church family who provided encouragement along the way; especially Larry, Pat, Celene, Jonathan, Shelly, and Samantha. Thanks also to the team at Thought Leader Academy and TLA Publishing who masterfully ushered me from prose to print: Sara, Marietta, Amy, Jill, Jane, Ed, Mike, JoAnna, Claudine, Liz, Erin, and Schamy. Thank you to Bridgette and Linda for directing me through our photography session and to John for producing my Times Square billboard design for the book. And thanks most of all to God for not giving up on me.